Penn Portraits
Further tales of Penn & District

Angus Dunphy OBE

First published 2016

© Angus Dunphy 2016

The right of Angus Dunphy to be identified as the author of this work has been asserted by him in accordance with the Copyrights, Designs and Patents Act 1988.

British Library Cataloguing in Publication Data

ISBN 9781 911309 031

Design by David Leverton

Typesetting by Mike Pearson
E: editor@blackcountrysociety.co.uk

Printed and bound by Russell Press:

Russell House,
Bulwell Lane,
Basford
Nottingham
NG6 0BT

Dedication

For Jon Everall and Alf Russell

and all who work at Wolverhampton City Archives in Molyneux House

Wedding party at Molyneux Hotel, 1920s

The Black Country Society

The term 'The Black Country' was coined in the mid-19th Century to describe that area of the South Staffordshire coalfield where the 'thick coal' lay.

Over 150 square miles some 100 small industrial communities developed and by the late 1890s a couple of dozen of them were of sufficient size, perhaps when linked with some of their neighbours, to have their own local councils. Since that time there have been several local government reorganisations and after that of 1974 all of the townships of the Black Country were absorbed into the four Black Country Metropolitan Boroughs of Dudley, Sandwell, Walsall and Wolverhampton. In December 2000 Wolverhampton was granted city status.

The Black Country Society was founded in 1967 by enthusiasts, led by Dr John Fletcher, who felt that the Black Country did not receive its fair share of recognition for its great contribution to the industrial development of Britain and the world.

The Society grew out of the Dudley Canal Trust Preservation Society which had successfully campaigned to save Dudley Canal Tunnel which had been threatened with closure by the British Waterways Board and British Rail. The preserved tunnel linking the Birmingham Canal System and the canals of the Stour Valley, with links to the River Severn, is now a major attraction at the Black Country Living Museum.

The stated aim of the Society is to "foster interest in the past, present and future of the Black Country". Its voice calling for the establishment of a local industrial museum at a meeting on 6 October 1968 was one of the first on the subject.

In 2017 the Society celebrates its 50th anniversary and is still thriving, holding regular meetings and talks at two venues. We continue to publish books and other publications, with three or four new titles being launched each year. Our quarterly magazine, *The Blackcountryman*, is a well-respected journal, which contains authoritative articles from authors from around the world, no one is paid for their submissions.

For more information visit our website at: www.blackcountrysociety.co.uk

Contents

Foreword

Penn Portraits is an attempt to secure for future generations the history of Penn, before aspects are lost forever. The oral tradition of passing on knowledge usually dies out within a generation or two. This book gives a view of past sections of Penn society, showing how each lived their lives and how each met the challenges that faced them.

A year's research has recreated the fascinating story of Bearnett House on Lloyd Hill, from its origins as Dr Topham's Puttley Villa through the years of the ironmaster landowners the Wards, to its heyday under Frederick Harold Reeves. A rare glimpse of its rich past is portrayed through family photographs which display some amazing scenes. There is even a link from Penn to Peru!

Penn Court, its owners and times, is remembered before it succumbed under an expanded Wolverhampton, to be reinvented as Osborne Road. The parish of Upper Penn within Staffordshire ceased to exist in 1933. Manor Road Senior School, opened in September 1932 by Staffordshire, also was transferred into Wolverhampton Borough on April 1st 1933.

Man has lived on the river terraces of the Smestow Valley for ten thousand years. Farming is still active in South Staffordshire, as the chapters on barns and Furnace Grange show. The latter story gives an exciting insight into the 17th century iron industry, which used water power to drive the bellows for a charcoal blast furnace.

The agricultural lands to the west and the farming communities are covered by chapters on The Showell and Orton Hall. The reader can follow their story before it's lost as a new breed of country-dwellers take up residence. The natural history of the area is represented by chapters on the rook, owl and sparrowhawk. Angela Scott's diaries provide a record of late 1940s Wolverhampton as it emerged from the deprivations of the Second World War.

Penn Portraits also takes a quick look at Owain Glyndwr's campaign of 1404-5. It reminds us that had he taken bolder decisions at Worcester then all our futures may have been very different. Pattingham could well have been in Wales and Wolverhampton a border settlement!

This book does not seek to portray bygone Penn through rose-tinted glasses, for there never was a perfect age. Life for most of our forebears was hard – a struggle to feed, clothe and provide shelter for their families. There was no welfare state, state education system or access to free medical advice and support until well into the modern age. Even the well-to-do did not escape the serious illnesses associated with 19th-century industrialisation and population growth. Most people seem however to have lived a fulfilled life in Penn. For most it was lived at a slower pace: it was simpler, less demanding, but much more physical. The sense of community was much stronger as the populace lived closer together and shared in the major annual events, which were usually linked to the seasons and to the church.

The book allows you to make comparisons with the past and to analyse the factors that have brought about change. What is certain is that we will continue to experience change as we adjust to international market economies, as the patterns of our society alter over time, and as our land is used in different ways for different purposes. So read on and enjoy a journey back through time.

Angus Dunphy   Dinas Powys, 2016

Acknowledgements

In writing this latest book I have again had the support of a large number of people and I freely acknowledge their help and advice.

The story of Bearnett House took a year and more to reconstruct and it would not have been possible without the family archives of Mrs Jocelyn Hayward, Mrs Wendy Veazey, Mr Phil Oliver and Miss Diana Vaughan – grandchildren of the house's former owner Frederick H Reeves. Mrs Jane Elcock provided photographs of Bearnett in the early 1920s, whilst Mrs Helen Willis, the owner of Bearnett House Residential Care Home graciously allowed me free access. Mr Patrick Walker gave me the encouragement to start the task, whilst Mr George Miller and Mr Tom Clarke, both Rolls-Royce enthusiasts, provided the breakthroughs which allowed the tracing of Frederick Reeves' first Rolls-Royce to Peru. Mr Jorge Nicolini, owner of South America's most important motor museum – Museo del Automovil Coleccion Nicolini – generously provided the photographs of the restored Rolls, reg. ARE 400. If you are in Lima the museum is a must visit. I have tried and regrettably failed to contact Mr Hernan Cortes MacPherson (MacPhotography), who photographed the car in the Lima workshops of the Museo in 2012, for permission to reproduce that picture, which appears among his images on the photo-sharing website Flickr. A direct link to it on there is available, however at:

www.flickr.com/photos/macstudio/8081848592/in/album-72157631756882784/

Mr Peter Creed's interest in Penn Court prompted me to update what we know of the former house and its owners. As always the photographs of Graham Adderley add depth to the text in this volume, particularly in the chapter on Orton Hall. Some black & white images from Stephen Price Associates Ltd's 2009 report 'Outbuilding at Orton Hall Farm' are also gratefully used in that chapter. David Leverton's excellent sketches enhance several of the chapters.

The piece on The Showell was written for the family of Leonie Menezes (née Marston) who was brought up on the Orton Hills and who loved its wildlife and vistas. She died in Ontario in July 2015 – a much loved mother, sister and a gifted all-rounder. Anne Brown and Eleanor Whatmore provided the photograph of their grandfather Thomas and his wife Alice Pace outside Rose Cottage, Showell Lane.

Mr and Mrs Inett graciously made me welcome at Furnace Grange Farm, whilst the earlier works of Dr Peter King and Derek Thom allowed me a fuller understanding of the property's development.

I am grateful to Mrs Gill Skitt for permission to reproduce the photograph of Fletchers' shop on Sedgley Road, Penn Common. I am also grateful to May Griffiths MBE, the Wombourne historian, for details on the old motorbus body which was once located at Bullmeadow.

The aerial, satellite view in the Triangle Piece chapter is courtesy of Google, whose Google Earth imagery may be freely used in moderate quantities within limited-distribution works such as this one.

David Leverton has skilfully formatted the work and Mike Pearson, the editor of *The Blackcountryman*, was again kind enough to do the typesetting and organised the printing.

Lastly, but by no means least I acknowledge Mr Alf Russell and Mr Jon Everall of Wolverhampton Archives, to whom this book is dedicated. Their support for researchers is of the highest order. They go about their business quietly and calmly and their efficiency and support shines through. The City possesses not only a wonderful resource but a fine historic building in Molyneux House, in which to carry out research. The menu card, William Hanbury Sparrow's portrait and the Osborne Rd house plan in the Penn Court chapter are all courtesy of the Archives.

I apologise to anyone I have failed to acknowledge, but you too will have had a hand in bringing *Penn Portraits* to fruition. The copyright of photographs other than those taken by Angus Dunphy remains with those persons credited. I hope I have included everyone.

Bearnett House from the southeast (above) and south (below), 1981

Former swimming pool, looking west to Orton Hills ridge (below)

Bearnett House on Lloyd Hill, Penn, began its new career as a nursing and care home in 1987. At the time of the first edition of the Ordnance Survey in 1834 the site was still a field. The OS map was based upon surveys completed between the years 1814-17 and extensive re-surveys in 1831/2. Neither was there any evidence of buildings at the time of the Penn Tythe Survey of 1843. Indeed, the eight acres of field number 617, which was known as 'Putley', was down to arable crops. It was owned by the executors of the late Thomas Bate and farmed by Sarah Bate. Thomas Bate had been a large landowner in Penn, holding parcels of land in the south, at what was to become part of the Bearnett, Earlswood and Foxlands Estates, whilst in the north of the parish he held Leasowes House and lands in Merry Hill, Pinfold, Coalway and Pennfields. All in all Thomas had owned some 210 acres. Even as late as the 1851 census there was no substantial dwelling at Bearnett, although a George Pilsbury, a gardener, is listed as living somewhere in Putley in his cottage.

In the years that followed Dr John Topham built Puttley Villa on the site of what is now Bearnett House and he was living there in 1860. He was the South Staffordshire General Hospital and Wolverhampton Dispensary's – later renamed The Royal Hospital – first physician (1849-1887) and a Fellow of the Royal College of Physicians. The Cleveland Road site opened its doors in 1849 and was supported by voluntary subscriptions and donations. Dr Topham was also the honorary physician to the early boarders at the Orphan Asylum. It took over the Dispensary building in Queen Street in 1850, but with increasing admissions it moved to new premises on the Penn Road in 1854. It was eventually to become the Royal School. The building of Bearnett House has been given a date of 1854 and this probably refers to Topham's earlier residence. The Bearnett that we know is a building of architectural merit, Grade 2 listed, and built in the Elizabethan style in mellow red brick with stone dressings. The main elevations are characterised by ogee gables and mullioned windows with leaded casements and ornamental copings. The house has an impressive portico and entrance hall beyond which is an equally impressive main staircase. Most of the downstairs principal rooms have wooden panelling.

Below-stairs the cellars, which probably date in part from the earlier Puttley Villa, were once extensive and lay beneath a much larger Bearnett House. They were rickety by the time of the Second World War, when they were used as an air raid shelter. One of the Reeves family stated that she would rather take her chances above ground than be buried alive! The servants' quarters on the west and north sides of the house were demolished about 1954/5. When the 1980s nursing/care home accommodation was increased on these aspects extensive cellarage was discovered and had to be filled in before the additional wings could be built. Today the cellars are limited in size and house the laundry and an unused boarded-up storage space. There is a story of secret passageways, as there is about many pre-twentieth century large houses: the cellars, it is claimed, were once connected to the folly tower which lies to the south of the house, and which is today in one of the bungalow gardens. This is not so as the remaining cellarage has been examined and it has been found to lie within the bounds of the house. The slight depression in the lawns may have been caused by the original water feed to the former circular pool with fountain, and to the former swimming pool, again with a central fountain.

East elevation, 1920s, before the property was reduced in size in the 1950s (top), and today (above)

Demolition of the servants' accommodation in progress (left)

It was George Ward, a Staffordshire ironmaster and a county JP, who first built the house as we know it. He was living there by 1864, with his wife Ann Lydia, the daughter of S Barnett of Comberton, Worcestershire. They had married in 1855, but don't appear to have had any children. In 1891 it required seven servants ranging in age from 16 to 62 years to run the house and meet their every need. George also owned Heath House, Wombourne and from the West Staffordshire Poll Book of 1868 we know that he voted from there, unsurprisingly for the two Conservative candidates, Ingram and Childs, who were duly elected to Parliament. George was also responsible for creating Bearnett's sylvan setting; an early twentieth century book notes that the house was *"picturesquely situated in the vicinity of Wolverhampton"*.

The Wards had built their wealth on the South Staffordshire iron trade from the time of the Napoleonic Wars. George's father William Ward had entered into a partnership with Samuel Fereday and Richard Smith at the Priestfield Furnaces at Bilston. When the partnership was dissolved in 1819 William bought out the other interests, and developed the site which included blast furnaces, foundries, casting houses and coal and ironstone mines. Tram roads connected the mines to the blast furnaces and to the Wolverhampton canal. Once the minerals were worked out the Wards had the foresight to extend operations towards Willenhall and Portobello. William's two sons, Henry (1828-1904) and George (1833-1899) joined the business, it becoming known as William Ward & Sons. The company built a new works alongside the Walsall canal at Willenhall, and called it New Priestfield. William Ward was a member of the South Staffordshire General Hospital's board and it may have been this connection which prompted his son George to buy Puttley Villa.

The Wards were connected to another family of ironmasters, the Bagnalls, who owned Gold's Green furnaces at West Bromwich and Capponfield at Bilston – Henry married Jane Bagnall in 1855, whilst his sister Mary married Jane's brother John Nock Bagnall. John had Dud Dudley's *Metallum Martis or Iron made with pit-coale*, dating from 1665, reprinted in 1854 and H Ward was one of the subscribers. Henry Ward was High Sheriff for Staffordshire in 1872, a JP and Deputy Lieutenant for Staffordshire. He lived at Rodbaston Hall, Penkridge. Henry and Jane had a son, Henry Herbert Ward, in 1857. On George's death in 1899 Bearnett was left to his nephew.

George and Ann Ward's graves in St Bartholomew's churchyard

The nearby fields carry the names of Big, Far, Long, Wild, Little Wild, Spring, Lower, Near and Bagnalls Putley. The latter named field probably refers to the link between the two families, but it is difficult to explain its derivation unless Bagnall was added after the Wards bought Bearnett, which was well after the tythe survey of 1843.

Documents from the medieval period which refer to the 'Putte de la Lude', 'Putterley', 'Puttesley' and 'Pit of the Lloyd' help draw attention to the word *Putte*. A putte is a narrow neck of land which joins two larger masses and in this case the Bearnett/Putley district is just that. Up until the boundary revisions of 1934 Bearnett was the link between the main part of Lower Penn parish lying to the north and the district of The Lloyd, which stretches down to the Wodehouse mill pool. In the medieval period the Wood of Putley, which stretched across the Orton Hills, was part of Kinver Forest and was rich in game – but hunting was reserved for the King. There is ample evidence of felons brought before the forest courts for stealing the royal venison. In 1286 two cases were tried, but we do not

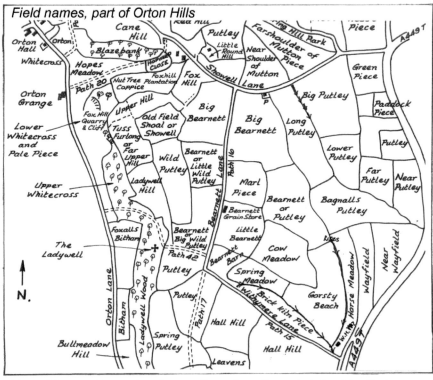

Field names, part of Orton Hills

Map of Lower Penn showing north and south parts joined by Putley

know how the men fared. It is likely they escaped with large fines. These types of case were fairly regular occurrences as local men, often well-to-do, chanced their luck. In 1272 Ralph Drulle with the King's verderers came into the wood and took a doe and on another occasion a roebuck. Ralph made the mistake of not attending the forest court to which he had been summoned, so the sheriff was despatched to make him attend. He was committed to prison, but was brought out and fined one mark. Pledges were also given by Warin de Penn and Richard Gervase of Wolverhampton as to his future good behaviour. In the same year a large group of local men including William de Wrottesley and his brother Hugh, Nicholas of the Lloyd and his brother Thomas, and William son of Alice of Penn stole into the Wood of Putley on 22nd July. They shot and killed a stag, carrying the venison to the home of Alditha of the Lloyd, before dividing up the spoils. Prison resulted, but again fines were imposed and pledges given. Only William, son of Alice escaped punishment as the court decided he was too poor. The fines went to swell the King's exchequer.

There were other offences committed by local people. The most common included taking a piece of land from the wood without the King's warrant and sowing it with crops, usually oats. For this offence William de la Putte de Lloyd was fined two shillings and eleven and a half pence in

4

1262. Richard, the Vicar of Sedgley was also fined for a similar offence, as was Thomas de la Putte of the Lloyd. The land would revert to the King but often was rented back to the villager. One can understand the action of those offending as in many cases they would get two or three crops from the ground which would help with their winter food supply. Other offences included wasting the wood. So, William of Orton, who cut down the trees for their timber, was fined. The Court Rolls tell us that William and his ancestors had been doing this for a considerable time.

The word Bearnett refers to the fifteenth century Lords of Lower Penn, the Burnetts. Again several adjacent fields carry the name, Bearnett as well as Big and Little Bearnett. George Ward, a Victorian gentleman, would have found it fitting that his estate and social position carried a link with former Lords of the Manor. Position was everything in Victorian society and George ensured that his visitors would note his status. The coats of arms in the stained glass windows and on the wooden panelling above the fireplace in the library would have painted a fictitious picture of the family's glorious past.

Bearnett's grounds included a small lake around which were well timbered and shrubbed walks, which stretched around the north and eastern aspects of the property (today's lake and Water Gardens residences and Fairlawns, with its canal-based water garden). Conveniently situated close to the house and adjacent

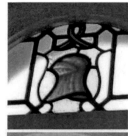

Stained glass at Bearnett House

Three-arch portico (below) plus its two side panels (l/r)

Residents' lounge, previously the drawing room (above)

The library, formerly the morning room (above)

The dining room's six leaded lights (above and below)

Resident's bedroom, formerly the study (below)

to the field boundary, was the stable and garage block (now a private residence). This was set around an enclosed square yard, the buildings ornamented by a handsome clock and bell tower. The horticultural buildings included two greenhouses of approximately 60 x 12 feet and 60 x 9 ft respectively as well as a lean-to peach house 81 x 12 ft. In these orchids, bananas, peaches, vines and a great variety of flowers were grown, thus making a strong statement about the owner's status. A stone path passed by the octagonal tiled gazebo and through the Japanese rock garden linking the house to the outbuildings.

The south-facing lawns gave way to a large formal rose garden encircled by a clipped yew hedge with a central feature of a circular lily pond and fountain. Beyond lay a swimming pool, again with central fountain with a figure and basin. Towards the field boundary was the folly tower and even a pets' graveyard. One stone, probably commemorating a favourite dog, read *'Rough 1911'*. To the west lay a partly-walled fruit and kitchen garden. To the east was ornamental stone balustrading with steps down to further formal gardens and a canal-featured water garden.

There were two lodges on the estate, one on Lloyd Hill at the entrance to Bearnett Drive, the other in Showell Lane. The latter was the head gardener's house. In those days there was a cartway from Showell Lane (from no. 51) to Bearnett and Lloyd Hill, which the gardener would have walked daily. Whilst the lodge, no.65 Showell Lane, has been extended its outward appearance still reflects the style of Bearnett. Ernest Rogers was the head gardener in the period at the end of the Great War and before the house was sold. He was responsible for keeping Bearnett's grounds in pristine order and for the fine display of orchids, which were his pride and joy. It is thought that for a time his wife was a cook at the house. Their daughter was named Agnes.

The farm access lane, Bearnett Lane, breaks away from Showell Lane near to the crest of the ridge, with its trig point at 550 feet. The farm buildings, which could be seen from the house, have now gone. They probably dated from the Napoleonic era, when extra land was brought into production as foreign markets were denied to Britain. The buildings included a large barn, beyond which were sheds and a labourer's cottage. For much if not all its working life the cottage was home to families of farm labourers, the farm being owned in the eighteenth century by Miss Mary Tongue, Orton's largest landowner. After her days Bearnett Farm was farmed in association with White Cross Farm at Orton and then from Orton Grange Farm. In the early 1930s William Vaughan, who came from a farm in Montgomery was the farm manager for Mr Wright. Subsequently William moved to a house at the Bratch.

Since the late 1950s Bearnett Farm has been operated as a cereal farm, with very large barley fields available to the contractor's harvester, but the removal of most of the hedgerows has led to loss of habitat for birds and small mammals, as well as to greater soil erosion to through-winds blowing during autumnal and March gales. Previously, water or the lack of it in dry weather was the major concern. In modern times a tractor would tow a water cart onto the farm. There was a cast iron pump in the cottage garden over a deep well, the sinking of which was a work of art – a perfectly cylindrical bore, cut into the sandstone. A very large and covered cistern gathered and stored any rainwater that fell on the cottage roof, whilst there were also two small farm ponds, one on either side of the lane. Another weather drawback was the farm's access in times of heavy snowfall. Snow would drift between the lane's hedges, sometimes making the access impossible for days on end.

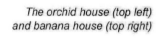

The orchid house (top left)
and banana house (top right)

One of the greenhouses (above left)

Boating on the lake (above)

The octagonal gazebo and
the clock & bell tower (left)

An adventure among the rooftops (left)

The folly (below)

Eastern aspect of the house over the terraces (below left)

Aerial view of the grounds (bottom)

Images from Reeves family cine film
shot at Bearnett House in 1936

Frederick 'Jimmie' Reeves diving into the swimming pool
to the south of the house (left)

Water spout from balustrade at terrace edge, southeast
corner of house (below)

The rose garden with its circular fountain, showing its
location in relation to the conservatory at the southwest
corner of the house (left)

Map showing Bearnett House, grounds and lake,
early 20th century (below)

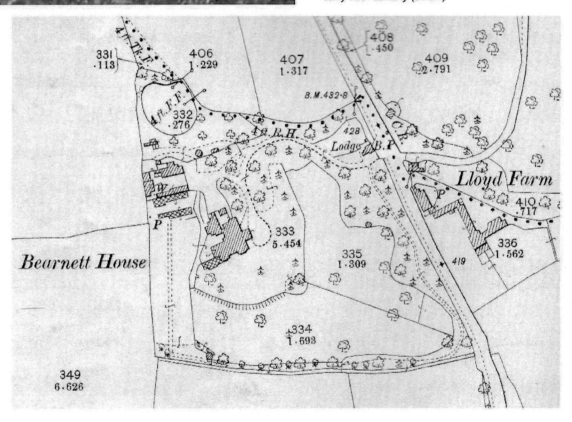

65 Showell Lane (Pen y Bryn) (top left)

and with chimneys removed, 1981 (top right)

65 Showell Lane as it is today (above)

Bearnett farm buildings, 1970 (above)

Bearnett Farm before demolition (right)

In 1901 the great Lloyd House sale took place, when Harriett Bradney Shaw-Hellier sold her 2115 acres. Many were bought by Henry Herbert Ward, giving him a holding of 1100 acres. He had been a Major (1897-1902) in and was an Honorary Lt Colonel of the 3rd Battalion North Staffordshire Regiment (Militia). Henry was also a JP for the county. In 1924 after his death (25th July, 1922) the estate, worth £58,862, passed to his nephew, Melville Hensman DSO, of Wingfield, Eashing, Goldaming, Surrey, a Commander in the Royal Navy. He was not a Midland man and his interests lay elsewhere. He therefore realised his assets and disposed of Bearnett. The estate's lands stretched from The Bratch to Ebstree, a considerable acreage which included rich farmland, woodland and land ripe for building homes.

It was thus that Mr FH Reeves purchased Bearnett House and grounds, moving from The Laurels in The Avenue at Upper Penn. The Laurels site was later to be incorporated into Penn Hospital. Frederick Harold Reeves owned Revo, the Tipton-based electrical fittings manufacturer. The company was named after its early partners – Reeves and Vaughan. It was a specialist in street lighting posts and fittings; the products having lasted are still on view in many towns. The Vaughans were near neighbours at Earlswood on the other side of the A449 and had at one time employed Frederick. They were edge tool manufacturers and subsequently developed Vono, the Tipton-based bed manufacturer.

Frederick H. Reeves

11

Frederick H. Reeves as a young man (above), and his signature (below)

Assembling electric cookers at the Revo works (above), and a wartime Revo auxiliary pump team in action (below)

Frederick was born on 2nd January, 1878 at Handsworth, to Mr and Mrs FA Reeves. His father was the warehouse departmental manager of a steel pen factory situated at 100 Charlotte Street, Birmingham, but he died when Frederick was just 16. His maternal grandfather was Thomas James Hart, a Birmingham gunmaker, whose works made breach-loading firearms. The address given was 65 Steelhouse Lane and 78 Lichfield Street in the city. The firm employed many men. Joseph Reeves who wrote one of the standard works on the history of West Bromwich was his paternal grandfather. Frederick had grown up with the expectation that he should make his mark in life. Necessity played a part too in his determination to succeed.

His first job was at a printer's office in Birmingham where he was paid 5 shillings a week. He was bright (attended King Edwards until he was 14) and prepared to work hard, so he quickly moved to a Walsall printer, Kirby and Sons as an office boy. From here he applied for the position of junior clerk stating he was skilled in book-keeping, shorthand, and French. He had acquired six months' experience of typesetting. A further move to Messrs Vaughan at West Bromwich gave him opportunity. In 1908, aged 30, he took the post of manager of Cable Accessories Co. Ltd using an almost derelict building of the old Etna Iron Works. He began with a few machines, and a small work force of no more than 12, making electrical joint boxes, feeder pillars and cable accessories. His annual wage bill was less than £1100. Frederick Reeves had vision. He could see that there was a great future in electrical lighting – for streets, motor transport and industrial plant. He foresaw the demand and began to plan for it. It was to bring him great wealth.

By 1913, under Frederick's leadership, the company had become the Revo Electric Company Ltd and had a workforce of 200 at its Tividale, Tipton site. It had purchased 3.5 acres and begun a building programme to meet its expanding business needs. The Great War saw the company placed under Government control, producing electrical equipment for military camps and transport ships. In the slump of 1921 Revo invested even more heavily in extensions. It branched out into making electric cookers and further electrical fittings for ships, mines and railways. It put its crystal set on the market. Some 500 municipalities were supplied with street lighting and Wolverhampton was an important buyer of Revo's fixtures and fittings. In the family he was known as "The man who lit up New

York" as Revo supplied the city and the grid with much electrical equipment. He was invited as the city's guest and put up at the Waldorf to see the improvements that Revo equipment had made. He travelled by RMS *Queen Mary* and took Ida and his older children with him – Barbara, Jimmie and Wendy. However, he waited until after the maiden voyage just in case there was another *Titanic* moment. Trips to Canada, particularly Winnipeg, also secured orders for the firm.

Barbara, Jimmie, Wendy, Ida & Frederick in New York

As Britain began to re-arm in the 1930s, Revo secured Admiralty, Air Ministry and Government contracts. At the start of the Second World War, because of its importance, it was again placed under government control. After the war Revo employed some 2500 workers, with an annual wage bill of £300,000, on a site of 22 acres and there was still a further 18 acres for expansion. Its annual turnover was 1 million pounds. The site was also geared to support employees in the use of their leisure time, with tennis courts and bowling greens amongst the facilities provided. Frederick had turned an industrial wasteland into a productive manufacturing plant which gave quality employment to thousands and which helped to re-invigorate the economy of Tividale and the wider West Midlands.

In just 30 years he had built an industrial empire. He was a self-made man, yet modest, finding pleasure in his family and home.

He suffered from a personal tragedy, for his first wife, Lilian Gertrude died suddenly in 1919. She was just 36. Her life is glowingly remembered by the fine Reeves memorial, which is found in St Bartholomew's Churchyard – an angel rising in glory, with the inscription *'Dearly Loved and Loving wife of Frederick H Reeves. A faithful wife and devoted mother. Oh for the touch of a vanished hand and the sound of a voice that is still'*. Their daughter Freda, who married into the Bedford Williams family of department store fame, is also remembered on one of the panels: *'Freda, the mother of John and Jennifer died suddenly on November 21st, 1956 aged 49 years'*.

Frederick subsequently married Ida Maureen Heath. She was 27 and he 43. She bore him six more children: Barbara Vivienne, born in 1921 was the eldest, and then in 1923 there was a son, Frederick Ernest, known as Jimmie – most of the children were given nicknames which were used by family

Reeves memorial

and friends. Ida Brenda, called Wendy, was born in 1924; Vanda Hilary, called Twink in 1927; Iris Patricia, nicknamed Paddy in 1929; and Joyce Rosemary, called Babe, in 1931.

Frederick's imposing portrait hung on the stairway above the entrance hall at Bearnett House, as did one of Ida, and it told something about his relationship with his children. His son, Jimmie, always addressed him as 'Sir'. Whilst Frederick was respected by his children, he was also loved by them.

Reeves family portrait at Bearnett, c.1936. Standing at rear: Frederick Ernest (Jimmie), Barbara Vivienne
Seated, middle row: Ida Brenda (Wendy), Ida Maureen, Frederick Harold with Iris Patricia (Paddy)
Seated at front: Joyce Rosemary (Babe) and Vanda Hilary (Twink)

He would sit with his youngest daughter and together they would invent stories about the scenes portrayed on many of the pictures hanging from the walls.

Babe was always happy in the house, playing hide and seek with her sisters in the spacious building and secreting herself away in the replica suits of armour in the entrance hall, or enjoying family parties on the lawns and bathing in the adjacent pond. A reel of cine film of 1936, which has miraculously survived, shows what an idyllic setting Bearnett was for the children. Swimming, cycling, tennis and riding ponies were all favourite pastimes in the extensive grounds. What impresses is how good the children were with each other. An electrically-powered child's car was also well used, whilst Jimmie at the age of 13 can be seen expertly chasing across the lawns in an Austin Seven

14

sports car. A lovely sequence of brother and sister, Jimmie and Wendy, racing across the southern paddock in a MG Midget sports car (registration LJ 7201) and on a horse would horrify today's health and safety police, but there is a gentleness portrayed by the car driver and a distinct bond between brother and sister having fun.

Tragedy struck Frederick's family once again when Vanda (Twink) died in the summer of 1937 from tuberculosis. She was just 10 and had previously broken her leg at boarding school. Her funeral was held at St Barts and a thousand roses from Bearnett's gardens lined her grave. Six Revo apprentices carried the coffin. Her mother Ida found Twink's death hard to bear, and perhaps this resulted in less structure and routine for her other children. Ida would have the chauffeur drive her to the graveyard in the Rolls-Royce. She would sit grieving beside the grave. She placed a line from the Irish blessing 'May the road rise up to meet you' on the gravestone – *'Til we meet again'*. In time both she and Frederick would join Twink. The other inscription on the memorial would certainly have given her comfort: *'Peace, perfect peace'*.

As a result of Twink's death the younger children were not sent to boarding school, but to the local school, St Bartholomew's. They found it difficult inviting friends back home to Bearnett: the house overawed its guests, its grandiose splendour being outside their experience. The younger Reeves children moved on to Bilston Girls High School, which was building a fine academic reputation.

Paddy was the 100 yards athletics champion, and Babe mirrored her achievement by regularly winning events at the annual Revo sports. Paddy became a notable horsewoman and won competitions from an early age. She took the prizes for the best-trained pony, the postman's race and the bending race at the Albrighton Hunt Pony Club Gymkhana in the 13–15 year old category. The event was held at Wrottesley Park and the prizes were presented by Lady Hickman. In adult life Paddy was a very well-known national show jumper, competing at the county shows as well as in the Horse of the Year Show at Harringay, which heralded the end of the equestrian season. She competed against Pat Smythe and in 1951 won the coveted British Show Jumping Association's National Championship on her horse Old Smokey. Paddy would be pleased to note that a further two generations of her family have competed at the Horse of the Year

Ida's portrait from the entrance hall at Bearnett (above), and Ida with some of her daughters at Rhyl (below)

Ida, Frederick and their daughter Twink are all commemorated on this memorial (above)

A young Paddy Reeves winning best-trained pony at Wrottesley Park (above)

Paddy astride her horse Old Smokey

Paddy's National Championship trophy (below)

Show. She ran a riding stable at Bearnett between 1949 and 1955 as well as teaching riding. She taught Jill Ireland the film actress, who has a star on the Hollywood walk of fame, to ride. Paddy was the last member of the Reeves family to reside at Bearnett.

As the children grew up they enjoyed the garden parties and sports held at Bearnett, through Frederick's generosity to the people of Penn. The Revo Electric Prize Band was a star attraction and was much appreciated throughout the afternoon and in the evening for the dancing. The older children had a wider exposure to the social scene of the 1930s and had much freedom. The Reeves children from an early age performed at the garden parties. That of 1936 saw them give a dance and ballet display to the invited guests who stood and sat on the lawns, thus making a perfect arena. Jimmie, as well as dancing, also played the accordion.

The Revo Prize Band was also a feature on Christmas morn when it played carols on the lawns at Bearnett.

The later pre-war garden parties were considered by some to have risqué elements, such as bathing beauty contests around the swimming pool. Alcohol was also available.

The importance of the house and the standing of its owners were demonstrated through their guests and acquaintances. The Reeves family mention that Lady May of Cambridge, a great granddaughter of Queen Victoria and niece to Queen Mary, stayed at Bearnett. Edward, Prince of Wales – the future King Edward VIII – would arrive in his car to transport her back south after his stay at Himley Hall; only after this were the Reeves children allowed to be seen and heard. There were other important connections. Ida was friendly with Rosemary, Viscountess Ednam, the only surviving daughter of the 4th Duke of Sutherland and wife to the future 3rd Earl of Dudley. Tragically Rosemary was killed in a plane crash in Kent in July 1930. It is thought that Ida called her youngest daughter Joyce Rosemary in honour of her friendship

BEARNETT HOUSE, PENN

• • •

Garden Party and Sports

BY INVITATION OF MR. & MRS. F. H. REEVES

JULY 20th, 1929, at 2.30

• • •

PROGRAMME

SPORTS

EVENTS

RUNNING (G. Williams)
100 yds. Flat, Men
75 yds. Flat, Ladies
Relay Race, Departmental,
            (Team of 4) Men
Relay Race, Departmental,
            (Team of 4) Ladies
Three-leg Race, Mixed

BOWLING (H. Hubble)
Bowling Tournament, all play from scratch

TENNIS (H. W. Taylor)
Men's Singles
Ladies' Singles
Mixed Doubles
FINALS ONLY. (Heats will be played off on the Revo Sports Ground.)

TUG OF WAR. (G. Jones)
Teams of 8, Departmental, Men
    ,,   ,,   ,,   Ladies

MUSICAL BAND RACE

NOVELTIES
Throwing the Cricket Ball
Football Place Kicking

• • •

A. C. REVILL, Chairman.   J. T. HOLDS, Secretary.

*Garden party programme, 1929,
and Frederick H Reeves with the
Revo Electric Works Prize Band*

Programme of Music

BY

Revo Electric Works Prize Band

• • •

AFTERNOON

March	" Avondale "	Verner
Selection	" Desert Song "	Romberg
Overture	" Raymond "	Thomas
Switch	" Comin' Thro' the Rye "	Truman
Fantasia	" Souvenir De Russe "	Rimmer
Selection	" Lilac Time "	Schubert
Musical Comedy	" Yes Uncle "	Nat Ayer

• • •

TEA WILL BE PROVIDED IN THE LARGE MARQUEE

• • •

EVENING

*All the latest Foxtrots and Waltzes for
Dancing.*

Jimmie playing the accordion outside Bearnett House, mid-1930s

with the Viscountess. In adult life Jimmie, it is said, was friendly with the actor Robert Donat and entertained him at Bearnett.

As the late thirties turned to war Jimmie, who had gained an MSc at Cambridge, joined up and worked in intelligence on the South Coast. The family tell of the part he played in the design of the Mulberry Harbour, so important for D-Day. Wendy became a 'Wren', a member of the Women's Royal Naval Service.

The grounds of Bearnett House seem to have been the venue for several visits by evacuees. These visits were organised by the Vicar of Penn; games and sports were played, but when Frederick returned from work the group made itself scarce.

Frederick's eldest daughter Barbara met one of the officers of the 15th battery of the 6th Heavy Anti Aircraft regiment, sited on Penn Common at the start of the Second World War. John Ross Seager of Liverpool had risen through the ranks and was a second lieutenant – and was to become her husband. They became engaged, but before the

romance could progress his unit was posted to Iraq. On the way they were diverted to Singapore, arriving there as it was falling to the Japanese. After many adventures he ended up in Java and with the Dutch surrender he was interred by the Japanese, eventually working in the coalmines in Japan. Poor diet, lack of vitamins and ill health followed and he was not a well man by the end of hostilities. His journey home began in October 1945 on an American ship bound for Manilla. Eventually he reached Vancouver. A rail journey of five days across Canada took him to Halifax from where he set sail. He now wrote to his fiancée. It is difficult for us to realise the surprise this would have caused, for

Wendy as a Wren in the WRNS

Barbara did not know whether he was alive or dead. She had not heard from him for over four years, and neither had he heard from her.

They would have needed time to get to know each other again. He lived with a weak chest and needed ongoing medical treatment, but eventually they were able to marry in 1946. The wedding party photograph below was taken on the lawns outside Bearnett House. Frederick invited him to join the board of Revo. Over the ensuing years Barbara and John raised two daughters, but they did not live at Bearnett, moving to a cottage in Wombourne before leaving the district for Bishampton in Worcestershire.

Barbara Vivienne Reeves marries Lt. John Ross Seager, 1946, photographed on the lawns at Bearnett House. l-r: Wendy Reeves (sister of the bride), Jessie Seager (mother of the groom), Arthur Steed (best man), Ina Seager (sister of the groom), the bridegroom and bride, parents of the bride Frederick & Ida Reeves, unknown bridesmaid (friend of the bride)

Frederick Reeves did not seek public life, preferring to spend his leisure time at Bearnett, collecting antiques and turning the house into a most desirable residence. To us the house might have looked cluttered with an almost Victorian/Edwardian décor, but in this respect Frederick was a man of his upbringing. His collection of paintings was at least impressive, with some pieces of national significance. In 1938 Wolverhampton Art Gallery ran an exhibition of Victorian painters; Frederick lent paintings by five of the giants of the Victorian era. Amongst them was Sir Lawrence Alma-Tadema's *Roses of Heliogabalus* with its riot of rose petals, which received public acclaim. It is now owned by the Spanish-Mexican billionaire businessman Juan Antonio Perez Simon. Also displayed were works by the same artist entitled *Water Pets* and *The Armourer's Shop*. Other works represented were Frank Cadogan Cowper's *Venetian Ladies Listening to a Serenade*, Sir Edward Poynter's *On The Temple Steps*, Lord Leighton's *Magic of the Sea* and Dante Gabriel Rossetti's *Dis Manibus*. The system of individual lighting used was that which Frederick had developed at Bearnett House. At the same time Frederick gave the Gallery a large oil painting of 1846 by Ary Scheffer, *The Vision: Dante and Beatrice*.

The size and importance of what he had collected in the house is reflected in the sale organised by his executors, which lasted for three days in July of 1953. The sale brochure announced:

> "Chinese, Axminster, Persian and Turkey carpets and rugs; carved oak dressers, tables, cabinet and refectory table, sets of walnut and mahogany dining chairs in the Caroline, Adam and Chippendale styles, full compass Steinway Pianola-Piano, carved mahogany sideboard suites and dining tables; grandfather, lantern and other clocks; small collection of armour and weapons; small library of books; collection of specimen pewter and copper ware; valuable bronzes and enamels; finely carved ivories; decorative and domestic china and glass; costly bedroom appointments; lead and stone garden figures, vases and ornaments".

But his paintings and pictures were the real gems of the sale. Amongst the paintings sold were works by Alma-Tadema, Cowper, Leighton, Rossetti, Walter Dendy Sadler, Walter Langley, John Seymour Lucas, Ernest Crofts, Walter Osborne, WP Frith, Laslett J Pott, Bernard Munns, JW Waterhouse, WJ Wainwright, A de Andreis, Carl Bonifazzi, J Pratt, and Daniel Maclise. The post-war years were the ones in which to buy. If the sale had occurred in the 1970s or '80s, or even in the '60s it would have reaped bigger rewards for the family. In the event, it made ten thousand, one hundred and fifty nine pounds and sixteen shillings.

Another of Frederick's hobbies centred on his love of film. To this end he installed a perfectly equipped cinema in miniature. Nothing was lost on quality and there was a projectionist box complete with two up-to-date projectors and a stock of well-known movies. By arrangement with the film circuit distributors he was able to show the most recent releases. His son Jimmie was taught, and learnt to operate the projectors from an early age. Frederick's business and pleasure trips abroad were also captured on cine film, the ocean liner fulfilling the role of today's airliner.

Frederick Reeves' entrance hall at Bearnett House

*Some of Frederick Reeves' art collection,
sold at auction in July 1953*

Above:
Pastoral
  Lord Leighton

Top right:
A Suspicious Guest at *The Mermaid*
  J Seymour Lucas

Above right:
Breach of Promise
  W Dendy Sadler

Right:
Dis Manibus or A Roman Widow
  Dante Gabriel Rossetti

Cars seen at Bearnett in 1936 cine film

Two Rolls Royces: Sir Malcolm Campbell's Phantom II Continental saloon (above left) and a 20/25 6-light saloon of 1934 with coachwork by Crosbie & Dunn of Smethwick (above right)

Buick sedan (right)

Austin Seven sports car, chasing child-sized electric car with 'FER' plate for Jimmie's initials (below right)

Jimmie in MG Midget sports car with Wendy on a horse, in the southern paddock (below)

23

Mr FH Reeves with his 30hp, 8-cylinder Sunbeam

Frederick was clearly a very wealthy man with all the trappings that that provided. This can be seen in the range of cars that he owned. The photograph on the left shows a top of the range, luxury Sunbeam motorcar, made in Wolverhampton and which competed very favourably with the best models of all other car manufacturers. In Bruce Dowell's 2004 book *The Supreme Car: Sunbeam 1899-1935*, the same photo is reproduced stating Frederick's car was a 35-horsepower. This model was even more powerful, more prestigious and more expensive at well over £2000. Whether the car was a 30hp or 35hp matters little, as both would reference Frederick's standing. What is certain is that Bearnett provides a wonderful setting for both Frederick and the car. Dowell claims that Frederick commented that his Sunbeam had done 20,461 miles and was running as sweetly as the day he bought it. Dowell also quotes that altogether only sixty-five 30hp/35hp models were made during the production run from 1926-9, and that only four survive. Of these, one was for sale in April 2016 at Sotheby's for £200,000–£250,000.

Frederick's wealth and connections were further illustrated by the luxury cars that can be seen outside Bearnett House on the aforementioned reel of cine film taken in 1936. These included his Buick sedan, and two Rolls-Royces are also filmed coming up the drive.

Research reveals, remarkably, that one of these Rolls – registration AGO 1 – was a Phantom II Continental saloon (chassis number 140my) owned by the great land-speed and water-speed record breaker Sir Malcolm Campbell, who had purchased it from new in May 1933. This suggests that he visited the house, perhaps to use Frederick's expertise and contacts within the West Midland electrical and motor manufacturing industries. Sir Malcolm set a series of new world land speed records in the 1930s in his various vehicles named *Blue Bird*, at Pendine Sands in Carmarthenshire then Daytona Beach and the Bonneville Salt Flats in Florida, which peaked at 301 miles per hour in September 1935.

It is known that Malcolm Campbell was a visitor to the Sunbeam works and that he owned several Sunbeam cars, which he raced at Brooklands and at other tracks – his first two speed records were set in a Sunbeam. His Rolls-Royce AGO 1 was re-registered in Southampton in 1937 as CHO 980, and there is a suggestion that the car was given to the Royal Air Force, but that the registration number was retained by the Campbell family. By 1974 the car was registered to a Mr Smith in the USA and by 1983 it was being restored in Florida by Mr Mike De-Costa. After his death it was sold and brought back to Britain. In 2000 a Mr Diddle owned the car and he may have been the gentleman who re-imported it to Kent. It was probably at this time that it acquired its current registration number of 711 YUG. Eventually sold on, the new owner was responsible for its restoration and the current, appropriately blue livery. In December 2015 it was for sale at a showroom in Essex, with an asking price of £220,000.

That other vehicle seen driving in the film is a Rolls 20/25 four-door, six-light saloon, registration ARE 400, with Crosbie & Dunn Ltd coachwork. The latter were a Smethwick firm, operating from the Bearwood Road. Captain Crosbie, who was then employed at Flewitts, another coachbuilding firm, bought the premises of Davis and Hargreaves and with E Dunn set up the company. Crosbie & Dunn operated as coachbuilders between 1927 and 1939, the time when coachcraft was at its height and buyers would have their vehicles' bodywork tailor-made to their tastes.

ARE 400's particulars are: engine number J9K coming off test on 4th September 1934; chassis number GYD 38; and body number 136. Frederick registered the car on 15th October 1934 at Stafford, hence the registration prefix. The 20/25 may well have been underpowered for the undulating countryside around Wolverhampton.

The history of the car up to the early 1960s is unclear, but it was then imported into Peru by Mr Juan Manuel Colmenares. A prominent businessman, he was engaged in property development. When he died, his family inherited ARE 400, but the vehicle was left garaged for several years. In 2012 however Mr Johnny Schuler, manager and master distiller of the La Caravedo distillery in Ica, bought this Rolls-Royce for the company, which is owned by Messrs Bill and Brent Kallop and produces the pisco (brandy) known as Porton.

That year the car was photographed under restoration by Mr Hernan Cortes MacPherson in the Lima workshops of the Museo del Automóvil Colección Nicolini. It was very much recognisable as Frederick's original car. After its restoration ARE 400 has been moved to Ica, which is a wine growing region 300 kilometres to the south of Lima.

We know that Frederick subsequently purchased a new Rolls-Royce Phantom III saloon model, registration number DXM 471 with Park Ward bodywork and chassis number of 3 BU56, in March 1937. The photograph on the following page, showing this later car along with 20/25 saloon ARE 400 outside Bearnett with Frederick and his chauffeur present, must therefore date from no earlier than this. By 1974 DXM 471 was in the USA and owned by a Mr White.

Frederick Reeves' wife Ida died, at a relatively early age, at the Queen Victoria Nursing Institution at Chapel Ash on 19th February 1952. Frederick himself was not well, and a day and night nurse were engaged. He died in 1953 and the house and grounds were put up for sale.

In these years the house was not well maintained, though of the grounds one writer could comment:

"the house stands in 17.5 acres over half of which is a delightful garden, elaborately terraced and artistically planted, and having in it fountains, lily ponds, statues symbolic of the seasons, classical figures, a large bathing pool and rock garden."

Frederick Reeves (back right) and chauffeur with Rolls-Royce Phantom III reg. DXM 471 (at left), new in 1937, and 20/25 six-light saloon reg. ARE 400 of 1934, above.

Below is one of the very same cars, ARE 400, after its full restoration some 75 years later in the workshop of the Colección Nicolini at the Museo del Automóvil in Lima, Peru.

*The results of the restoration of the 1934
Rolls-Royce 20/25 saloon reg. ARE 400,
carried out at Lima's Museo del Automóvil
Colección Nicolini over a one-year period*

27

The sale particulars would foretell a future use of the house, when it stated it would be suitable as "a preparatory school or nursing or convalescent care home". Bearnett was offered for sale in four lots – the house and 8.75 acres; almost 5 adjoining acres to the south; a bungalow (where Harry the groom had lived between 1937 and 1947); and two adjoining acres to the north.

 At that time of the 1953 sale, the ground floor of Bearnett was described as comprising:

• *Triple arch portico leading to spacious entrance hall with Minton tiled floor, partly oak panelled walls with leaded light windows depicting armorial bearings. Leading from the centre of the Hall is   a wide oak staircase with carved oak bannisters;*

• *Drawing room* [today's residents' lounge] *with partly oak panelled walls, moulded cornice picture rail, handsomely patterned plaster ceiling, carved stone fireplace with over mantel, large leaded light French Bay windows with coloured coats of arms leading to the garden;*

Harry, groom from 1937-47,

PLAN

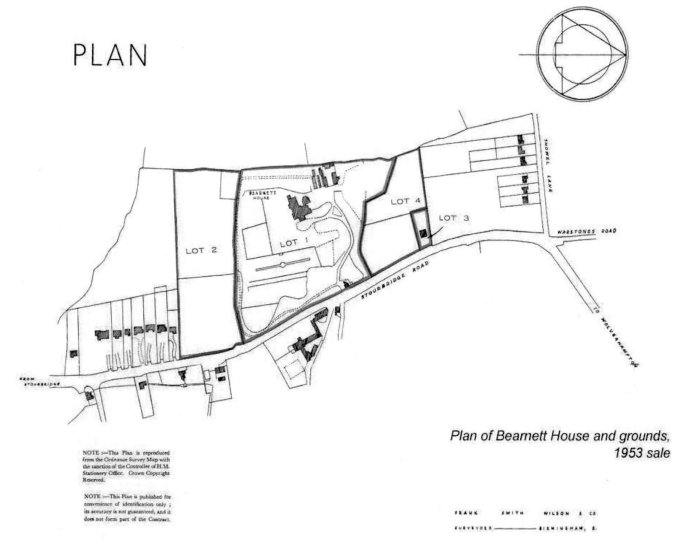

Plan of Beamett House and grounds, 1953 sale

NOTE :—This Plan is reproduced from the Ordnance Survey Map with the sanction of the Controller of H.M. Stationery Office. Crown Copyright Reserved.

NOTE :—This Plan is published for convenience of identification only ; its accuracy is not guaranteed, and it does not form part of the Contract.

FRANK   SMITH   WILSON & CO
SURVEYORS ——————— BIRMINGHAM, 2.

• *Dining room* [still the dining room] *with moulded cornice picture rail, patterned plaster ceiling, carved marble fireplace, two leaded lights French windows showing coats of arms;*

• *Study* [to right of entrance hall] *with green mottled fireplace, leaded light French window with coloured coats of arms;*

• *Approached by a corridor with Minton tiled floor and partly oak panelled walls, the Morning room* [today's library] *with polished oak floor, oak panelled walls, moulded cornice picture rail, leaded light bay windows with coats of arms and a concealed door, leading to,*

• *Lean-To-Conservatory with heating pipes and display stalls* [today's sun lounge];

• *Billiard Room with briquette fireplace and herring bone pattern hearth, moulded plaster ceiling with central lantern light, leaded light windows. There is an annex to this room which enables it to be used as a cinema* [today's corridor and residents' bedrooms]

• *Adjoining is a cloakroom and WC.*

The then domestic offices give an idea of the number of servants required to support the family in residence. The accommodation included a main kitchen, butler's pantry, larder, housekeeper's sitting room, back kitchen, boiler room, small boot room and extensive cellarage.

So as to accommodate a large family as well as house-guests there were eight main bedrooms and three bathrooms on the first floor. In addition there were three secondary bedrooms.

Bearnett House was bought by Mr Carding in late 1954/early 1955. He ran Quality Motors at the bottom of Worcester Street, Wolverhampton. As has already been noted he had the servants' western wing demolished, whilst completely overhauling and refurbishing the main part of the house to a high specification. After the death of neighbouring landowner Mr Wright in the late 1960s, he added Bearnett Farm to his holdings.

As late as November 1961, Jimmie (Frederick Ernest) Reeves was giving a lecture on "The causes and effects of Harmonics from Fluorescent Lighting Circuits" for the Revo Electric Company. The venue was the Station hotel in Dudley.

During the 1970s and 1980s the land surrounding Bearnett House was sold and the site developed into a small residential estate. In the early 2000s the modern house known as Southlawns sited near the lake was demolished, and together with land from some of the large gardens in Showell Lane, the exclusive Water Gardens residences were constructed. The great cedar alongside the field wall was felled. Bearnett Farm became part of the Wodehouse Estate and is now farmed with other lands by the tenant at Smallbrook Farm. Bearnett House itself began a new chapter as a luxurious care and nursing home, a role it continues to perform. A large oil painting of Bearnett House was donated by the Reeves family – including Frederick's daughter Wendy – to the Care Home and is now proudly displayed in the lounge, reminding residents of the splendours of the house and the role its owners have played in the Penn community and in the nearby conurbation.

Morning room, now the library (above left)   *Former morning room fireplace and oak surround (above right)*

Dining room with Chippendale-style furniture (below left and right)

Corner of the lounge (below left)   *Billiard room (below right)*

Position of Bearnett on Lloyd Hill, early 1970s

East elevation, 1981

Bearnett House from Orton Hills ridge

East elevation, 1981

Looking from Big Putley field east to Bearnett House, 1981

Frozen lake adjacent to Southlawns modern residence

31

1981, building bungalows at Bearnett

Fairlawns with canal and fountain

Oil painting donated by the Reeves family from Jimmie and his wife's estate to Bearnett House care home

Bearnett House, 1950

Wendy Adams (second right) with her son Mike Eadie and her two nieces Diana Vaughan & Wendy Veazey (far right), donating the painting to care home proprietor Helen Willis (centre)

View to Woodbury and Abberley Hills from the car-park

The view from Church Meadow field (St Bart''s Church car park) is one of the finest in the county. Away to the west the skyline is dominated by the hills of Woodbury and Abberley. They stand sentinel, as if in a face-off between Wales and England, and neither yields their ground.

In the gap between them lies Great Witley with its ruined Court, fountains and baroque church and of course the slender clock tower. It was said that the Earl of Dudley, from his seat at Witley Court, would brag that all that the eye beheld was his. A neighbour built the clock tower to remind him that there were others in this part of Worcestershire.

However, to return to the hills: they have many stories to tell, but the fifteenth-century one is the fight for Welsh nationhood, against the English attempt to secure strong monarchy. The main players in this drama were Owain Glyndwr – a member of the Welsh landed gentry and a man with a strong claim to the title 'Prince of Wales' on both his mother's and father's sides – and the English King Henry IV.

In many ways the late fourteenth and early fifteenth centuries was a period of changing values: a period when the old order was being challenged and when the old standards were beginning to loosen. It was a time when new ideas were beginning to permeate: a period when the Lollards challenged the established church, one that saw church reform from within, one that had experienced the ravages of the Black Death that brought tremendous social, economic and structural change in society; and it was a period in which the lawful King, Richard II, had been deposed and the crown usurped by Henry IV.

Owain Glyndwr was a lawyer, landowner, poet and supporter of the arts, and a talented and successful soldier with a record of supporting the English Crown. He had raised five sons and five daughters and of his daughters four had married Englishmen. His wife, Margaret, was the daughter of a judge of the King's Bench. To all intents and purposes he was an establishment figure, ensuring that the King's peace was kept between English and Welsh in Wales. He had learned to operate within the English laws. His family had surrendered their lands to the English Crown, receiving them back as tenants. The lands lay in three areas, the two main blocks being at Glyndyfrdwy with its centre at Carrog, and at Cynllaith Owain with its centre at Sycharth, near Oswestry. He also held land in Ceredigion.

Shakespeare in his play *Henry IV, Part 1* endowed Owain (as "Owen Glendower") with worthiness, affability, honour and intelligence, but he added boastfulness, which is not supported by the historical evidence.

Henry IV was reputedly the finest soldier in Europe, a cultured man and a generous patron to his friends. However, having usurped the throne he would spend the early part of his reign fighting with the Scots, Welsh, Irish and some of his barons to establish his writ and royal line.

In 1399 Henry IV called his first parliament in which Owain Glyndwr sought justice from his neighbour, Lord Grey of Ruthin, who had illegally taken some of his lands which lay on the moors above Ruthin and Glyndyfrdwy. The last time this had happened Richard II had supported Glyndwr, but now he was faced with a hostile parliament, whose members wished to show Henry IV their loyalty and seek his favour. Owain received little consideration as Lord Grey held the office of Chief Marcher Lord. Unlike earlier Marcher lords, who had gained their lands by conquest Grey had received his through purchase from the crown. A schemer, he sought to discredit Glyndwr in the eyes of the crown and failed to notify him in time of the King's writ to supply troops for a Scottish war.

At first Owain Glyndwr was a reluctant rebel. It was the inhabitants of Chester that lit the first spark of a revolt against Henry. A small group of family and friends met at Glyndyfrdwy and declared Owain, Prince of Wales. Glyndwr knew how to conduct guerrilla warfare; how to deepen the Welsh/English rift; how to appeal to the Welsh people through their bards and itinerant friars. The English parliament passed anti-Welsh laws which had the effect of reinforcing the divide and driving Wales into Owain's camp. In September of the year 1400 he burnt Ruthin, and in the following days attacked Denbigh, Rhuddlan, Hawarden, Flint, Oswestry and Welshpool. In 1401 he was the victor at the battle of Mynydd Hyddgen in Montgomeryshire.

Henry was stretched and short of money. He could only run a short campaign in Wales before he had to deal with troubles elsewhere. This contrasted with Owain and the year 1402. There was a comet in the sky that year, which the bards interpreted as his rising star as Prince of Wales. They gave him magical powers which frightened the English troops. Two centuries later Shakespeare continued the theme in his Henry IV part 1, when he had Owain giving this speech:

> 'To tell you once again that at my birth
>
> The front of heaven was full of fiery shapes;
>
> The goats ran from the mountains, and the herds
>
> Were strangely clamorous to the frightened fields.
>
> These signs have mark'd me extraordinary;
>
> And all the courses of my life do show
>
> I am not in the roll of common men.'

In this year he captured Lord Grey and Edmund Mortimer and won the battle of Bryn Glas near Pilleth in Radnorshire. Henry's civil war was beginning to spread and he made the mistake of ransoming Lord Grey yet not Edmund – the Mortimers had a claim of their own to the English throne through Richard II. This treachery would eventually lead to the Tripartite Agreement of 1405 between Thomas Percy, Earl of Northumberland, Edmund Mortimer and Owain Glyndwr, in which they agreed to divide England and Wales between them. Owain's share was a greatly extended Wales which followed the River Severn up to Worcester, before reaching the magical Six Ashes hamlet on the Kinver to Bridgnorth road, progressing to Pattingham, and thence northwards to the source of first the Trent and then the Mersey, and hence down the river to the sea. The agreement was more ideological than practical, but it did represent Owain's standing at the high point of his influence.

In 1404 Owain controlled all of Wales, except for Pembroke Castle and the large fortresses of the north, and his sphere of influence extended across the east bank of the River Severn: he held court at Harlech Castle and called his parliament to Machynlleth; he entered into negotiation for an alliance with the King of France.

This culminated in a French force landing at Milford Haven in 1405 and with Owain's forces taking Hereford and sacking Worcester. Owain now made a fatal error of judgement. He camped astride Woodbury Hill, an excellent defensive position, but one which lacked water and gave no attacking advantage. Henry checked him by camping on neighbouring Abberley Hill. Over the next eight days the stalemate reigned, only broken by individual knights from both sides coming off their respective hill to joust in the fields below and be killed in mortal combat.

Henry was the first to act. Overnight he slipped away to Worcester, where its walls gave him the advantage. Owain had missed his moment in history and had failed to defeat the English crown and set up an independent Wales. He crept back into Wales. The French left in 1406. Henry was now stronger with French and Scottish threats averted and unruly barons curbed. Over next few years Owain was a spent force; the castles were gradually lost and he could only operate through guerrilla tactics. He vanishes from history in 1413, probably dying in Herefordshire in 1415.

So the next time you are standing on the church car park, look out west and wonder how history might have been very different if Pattingham had been the border? Was Owain Glyndwr a patriot or terrorist?

Chapter 3
Make do and mend:
the strange afterlife of Corporation transport

They say necessity is the mother of invention. Our forebears certainly knew how to recycle and re-use manufactured goods. Little was wasted. In the case of a shortage of houses, a ready supply of old railway carriages, tram and bus bodies, and few if any planning restrictions led to some wonderful structures in our towns and countryside.

Up until 1960 the Bradmore railway carriage, a relic of Brunel's broad-gauge of 7ft, could be seen on the second floor of the house at 61 Victoria Road. Mr and Mrs Jones were the occupants of this

Railway carriage cottage, Bradmore

two-up and two-down structure. To the right of the doorway was the living room with its old fashioned fireplace in the gable-end wall; to the left a spacious kitchen. Upstairs the windows still gave it a feel of the trains, as some were operated in the railway fashion by use of a leather strap, whilst others were nailed shut. Headroom was limited, but it was a cosy home. Mrs Wright, the daughter of Mrs Jones reported that the family joke was that when Mr Jones, who was a smoker, went upstairs he would be told to go into the non-smoking compartment. This railway home had been built by her grandfather (Grandad Bowdler), who lived locally in the week, but who travelled away to his own home at weekends.

A number of other structures were dotted around our district. The Wolverhampton Corporation Act of 1899 gave the then town the powers to re-build existing tramways. The Corporation took over the horse trams from the Wolverhampton Tramways Company in 1900. Some 17 vehicles with a top deck, dating from the 1880s/1890s remained in service until the Lorain pole-less trams were introduced from 1902. One of the

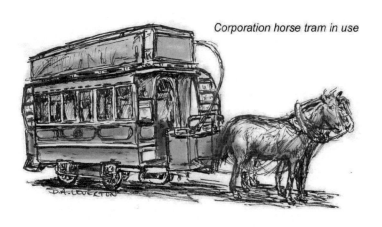

Corporation horse tram in use

horse trams, number 23 of the private company and re-numbered 15 by the Corporation, was sold for scrap and became a summerhouse in Seisdon. Today, fully restored by the British Horse Tram group in the 1990s, it can be found as part of the Black Country Museum fleet of public transport vehicles. It carried some 26 passengers in the downstairs saloon and about 18 upstairs.

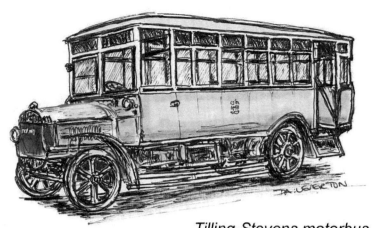

Tilling-Stevens motorbus

Mrs May Griffiths, the Wombourne historian, tells of her days at St Benedict Biscop School in Wombourne in the 1930s. During lunchbreaks she would play along the footpath which runs from School Road to Billy Bunns Lane. In those days this area was all fields, but where the footpath came out opposite Pickerills Hill there was a single-storey residence built from a bus/tram or train body. The fact that it was coloured brown with some cream suggests that it had been an early Tilling-Stevens motorbus, operated by Wolverhampton Corporation in the period from 1917 to the early 1930s. These vehicles were first painted brown, but later scarlet and cream. They remained in use until the late 1920s/early 1930s and carried approximately 30 passengers. A similar structure lay behind the Misses Partridge's shop in Langley Rd, Lower Penn, where it was used as a store-shed. Again there is evidence that the colour was brown or maroon and cream. By the 1970s a bungalow had been built on the site and the store-shed was swept away.

From 1923 Wolverhampton Corporation adopted the colour of apple green and primrose for their buses. The town became a pioneer of the trolley bus and its system grew to be extensive. The first trolley buses were purchased in 1923 for the Wednesfield route. Thereafter the town invested heavily in trolley buses, buying from two local suppliers – Guy and Sunbeam.

Guy (above) and Sunbeam (below) trolley buses

Sunbeam entered the market with its MS2 model in 1932, a three-axle bus with a twin rear wheel arrangement. The Guy BTX bus had a similar feature and was available from 1927.

The 1940s and immediate post-war years were difficult ones for bus operators and for the Corporation in particular. As factories were working 24 hours a day on war work there was a shortage of vehicles to transport workmen. Bournemouth Corporation loaned 16 trolley buses to

Wolverhampton in 1940; the last of the bright yellow vehicles were not returned until 1948. In the war years the Corporation issued special permits for factory workers doing night shifts. Others had to walk. Between 1947-9 the town hired additional motor buses from two local operators – Don Everall and Worthington Tours. Many of these vehicles were on their last legs. However, by 1950 new trolley and motor buses were becoming available and Wolverhampton added significant numbers to its fleet. This allowed the scrapping of many of the buses which were the mainstay of the 1920s/early 1930s. Several of these vehicles appeared in a new guise in the surrounding countryside.

The photograph below shows what is probably a Guy BTX in Trysull. The site may well be at Ebstree on the Seisdon border. The bus had been adapted as a residence on what was a smallholding.

There are at least three more examples of 1930s trolley buses finding a new life post-1949. A Guy BTX bus ended up at Seisdon as a storehouse. Another similar vehicle was to be found in a field somewhere in Wombourne parish, whilst a Sunbeam MS2 became a caravan in Seisdon. The precise location of these sites has faded from memory and as the structures have perished over time we may never know their locations. That is, unless you know differently!

The Black Country Museum has plans to recreate a bus home.

Sunbeam trolley bus home at Trysull

I spent my formative years on The Showell with its rural backcloth of fields, hedgerows, small watercourses and woodland. From late February through March, April and May until early June, I was always aware of our noisy neighbours- The Rooks. They are one of the eight members of the British crow family. In those days the A449T was a single carriageway as it struggled up Lloyd Hill, squeezing around the right-hand bend at the junction with Warstones Road, before finally reaching the Penn bus terminus at Springhill.

On the right-hand side of the road was Major Keay's Foxlands estate, dominated by tall elm, ash and sycamore trees. These provided the ideal site for a fine rookery, which was home to dozens upon dozens of birds. Their return in late February announced that spring was on its way (these days with global warming rooks return much earlier and depending on the season they are often evident in early January). The pre-dawn chorus of 'caw, caw, caw' provided an ever increasing cacophony of sound through the spring months, which would awaken me from my slumbers from 5am onwards.

The rook at about twenty inches long is unmistakable. Its black body is glossed with hues of blue, purple and green, but it is a bird of untidy appearance with feathers loosely hanging from its flanks and thighs. The greyish white face and dagger like bill are strong features. The rook is a sociable bird living in colonies and associating strongly with jackdaws as well as man, who can and often does provide a ready food source from his throw away attitude.

Nests were repaired and new ones built high up in the slender branches at the Foxlands. They were constructed of twigs, roots and sods of earth in an untidy way. And yet, when one blew down in a March gale and I was able to inspect it the inside structure was a work of art; for straw, grass, moss, dried leaves, hair and even wool lined the cup. Most trees contained many nests. A country saying records that if the rooks build their nests very high, then a fine summer will follow.

They are intelligent birds and are not adverse to stealing material from neighbouring nests. This led to squabbling and resulted in one of the partners remaining at their nest to repel robbers, whilst the mate brought in new material.

Five olive green eggs blotched with brown marks are laid in March. Like the Carrion Crow their eggs can vary in colour from green towards blue. The eggs are incubated for about three weeks by the hen bird, but once hatched both parents feed their young. The young birds remained in their nest for about a month, before taking their first flight. Spring all too quickly gave way to early summer and the experience of sharing their breeding season was gone for another year. The rookery was now strangely silent.

Rooks are not everyone's favourite bird. Noted for their sedentary walk, erect bodies and characteristic hop, they followed the plough as it turned over the soil, digging for wireworms; leather jackets (larvae of the crane fly), snails, millipedes and spiders. This contrasted with following the seed drill in the spring and late autumn, when they would pick up the grain as it was sown. Neither was their presence welcomed at the time of the potato harvest for much damage was done. The rook would also take young birds and eggs in the spring and feast on fruits and berries in the autumn. Farmers regularly shot the bird, as well as erecting scarecrows and mechanical devices to scare them away. The rich farmlands of south Staffordshire with their varied landscapes provided the rook with a perfect habitat

In the autumn I would watch large flocks of rooks scavenging on the fields for several hours. At this time of year they would also display their aerial skills in the strong winds. At dusk, like the jackdaw or starling they would leave it until the very last moment to come to roost. They seemed to shoot down on mass, descending in an oblique flight into the trees. Before finally settling down there was a burst of excessive noise as they jostled for the best roosts. Country folk refer to this feature as the 'winter parliament'.

With the sale of the Foxlands for housing and with the later dualling of the A449T's carriageways the rookery was lost and my relationship with them broken. Numbers nationally declined in the second half of the twentieth century due in part to post war housing need and road improvements, but also because of the loss, through Dutch Elm disease, of their favourite nesting tree. The greater use of chemical fertilisers by farmers killed off part of their food source, whilst global warming has presented new challenges to food supply. The rook is a clever bird and has found new larders. It has learnt to build its rookery next to many of our motorway services, which it treats as a 24 hour cafeteria. Its numbers are again on the increase.

The rooks from Penn moved for a time to the Foxhills at Battlefield on the Wombourne dual carriageway, nesting in the tall trees along the drive, but I for one miss our noisy neighbour, a bird with many positive characteristics and one which heralded the joys of spring.

Triangle Piece seen from the air   *Map data: Google Imagery*

The busy patch of ground, which lies between the Stourbridge Road, Warstones Road and Springhill Lane, is aptly named. Comprising a mix of Cooperative store, shops, vehicle repair centre and dwelling houses, its land use has drastically altered over the last hundred years. At the time of the Penn Tythe survey in 1843 (which mapped each piece of land and listed its owner, occupier, acreage and apportioned both the little and great tythe), Triangle Piece was listed as field 393, amounting to 5 acres 0 roods and 38 poles of pastureland. It was part of the Penn Hall Estate of William Bradney Purshouse (Persehouse) and was let to Thomas Clark. The little tythe was an annual payment payable to the Vicar and the great tythe to the Sub-Chanters of Lichfield Cathedral (and in a few cases to the Duke of Cleveland).

You will find the memorials to the Bradney/Purshouses on the south and north aisle walls at St Bartholomew's Church at Upper Penn. The Bradneys originated in Lower Penn, but became the local squires. You would have been sure to doff your cap to them as they passed in their smart carriage. At this time their estate extended to 561 acres and was the third largest landholding in the ancient ecclesiastical parish, which included both Upper and Lower Penn townships and stretched from Furnace Grange in the west to Penn Common in the east, and from the mill pool at Wodehouse Farm in the south, to Castlecroft, Finchfield, Bradmore and Goldthorn Hill in the north.

The Lord of the Manor was His Grace the Duke of Sutherland, who held 631 acres, whilst the Reverend William Dalton of The Lloyd, that grey ashlar-fronted house lying to the east of the dual-carriageway on Lloyd Hill, owned a massive 896 acres. These three landowners possessed 52% of the parish's land, whilst a further nine – Lord Wrottesley 521 acres; Earl of Dudley 125 acres; Thomas Higgins Burne of Penn Villa (later Woodlands site) 113 acres; William Jones, gentleman farmer 91 acres; William Thacker of Muchall Hall 85 acres; Joseph Tarratt of Castlecroft House 74 acres; Thomas Shaw-Hellier of The Wodehouse 56 acres; the Vicar of Penn 53 acres and Anne York, farmer, 52 acres – between them held another 29%!

If we add another dozen small landowners, who were mainly farmers and who held 225 acres between them, we can account for a further six percent of Penn's 3986 acres. Roads and waste made up another 5%. As can be seen most of the population were merely occupiers of their land, either Lady Day tenants or simply labourers.

William Bradney Purshouse died in 1843 and his heir, Henry, whose interests lay elsewhere, let Penn Hall – first to John W Sparrow the Black Country ironmaster and then to William Underhill, an important national iron stockholder. William died in 1899. It had been more than fifty years since a Persehouse had lived in Penn and George Persehouse placed the much reduced estate (388 acres) on the market. The sale took place at The Star & Garter Hotel in Victoria Street. Lot 12, of 3 acres 0 roods and 38 poles, included three fifths of Triangle Piece and was advertised as "valuable accommodation or building land". John Jenks of Penn Moor Farm was the Lady Day tenant and he had continued to use it as pasture for his sheep and cattle. The western portion of Triangle Piece had been sold sometime in the previous 50 years to The Lloyd Estate. They now purchased Lot 12.

However, Triangle Piece was to feature in a further sale within two years, reminding us that change is an inevitable and perpetual feature of our lives. Harriet Sophia Bradney Shaw-Hellier (née Marsh), the owner of the great Lloyd Estate of 868 acres had married Colonel Shaw-Hellier, of The Wodehouse, at a society wedding at St James' Church Piccadilly in 1899. Whilst it was a mutually beneficial match in terms of land holdings the marriage was not a success. Colonel Shaw-Hellier, already elderly, had formerly served with the 4th Dragoon Guards and afterwards had become Commandant of The Royal Military School of Music at Kneller Hall. A cultured, quiet man, he was remembered for breeding Jersey cattle and for being responsible for staging the Military Tournament at the Agricultural Hall in Snow Hill, Wolverhampton. He retired to San Giorgio at Taormina in Sicily. Harriet, a strong-minded individual in an age when society believed that 'a woman's place was at

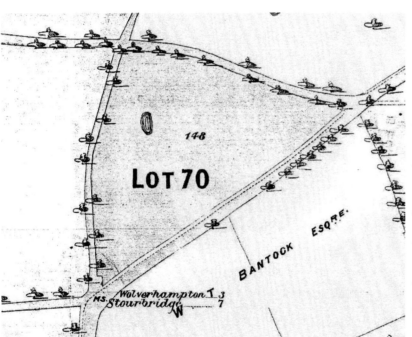

home', had insisted on retaining her property rights after marriage and had built them into the marriage contract.

In 1901 she chose to sell off The Lloyd Estate. Lot 70 – Triangle Piece – was advertised as "freehold accommodation meadow land with a total road frontage of 670 yards". Farmer Jenks was still the Lady Day tenant paying £9-10-0d annually. The sale map showed a farm pond, which may have been excavated in previous times for its marl for use as a fertiliser or for brickmaking, whilst it fulfilled a useful drinking spot for livestock. Current residents living on Triangle Piece will attest to the clayey nature of the soil, the deposits of boulder clay being laid down at the time of the last retreating ice sheet.

Much of the Estate was purchased by John Roderick, gentleman, and Joseph Bennett Clarke, a solicitor of Birmingham. They were property speculators. Triangle Piece was sold on to John Hope Shepherd for £528 and within three years it was sold again, this time to local entrepreneur James Lakin. A County Councillor, businessman, property developer and local worthy, he had 'a finger in many pies'. Some said he looked like the future George V. He rode on the Common in the annual races and was responsible for the castellation of the old brewery tower on the Common and also Carlton House on the Colton Hills. There he introduced stained glass, which provided a rainbow of colours when the sun shone, antique mosaic tiles in the long hallway and a fine plasterwork ceiling in the dining room. He also 'beautified' the Castle and Orchard property on Church Hill. He fought and lost an expensive legal battle over the roadway he had built across common land on Penn Common to Grassholme.

Lakin had a nose for profit. He bided his time and gradually as the market was ready sold off plots within the triangle. (The following list covers just over an acre. There are 4840 square yards in an acre):-

In August 1912 450 square yards were sold to Frank Short Clarke;

In December 1913 1860 square yards were sold to Jane Horton;

On 7th August 1914 662 square yards went to Thomas William Hughes;

On 16th November 1914 1268 square yards were sold to Frank Short Clarke;

On 23rd January 1918 500 square yards with a frontage to Springhill Lane of 10yards was sold to John Frederick Scott (Rose Cottage site);

In September 1918 a piece with 15 yards frontage to Springhill Lane was sold to Frederick Harold Reeves, a Tipton manufacturer, of The Avenue, Upper Penn for £55-12-6d. A dwelling house was eventually built on the plot and was called Virginia Cottage, latterly The Cottage. Reeves moved to Bearnett House in 1924 and sold Virginia Cottage for £400 to George Mason, the grocer, of The Woodlands. He probably used it for one of his workmen. At the time of the sale Alfred Deans had lately been the tenant.

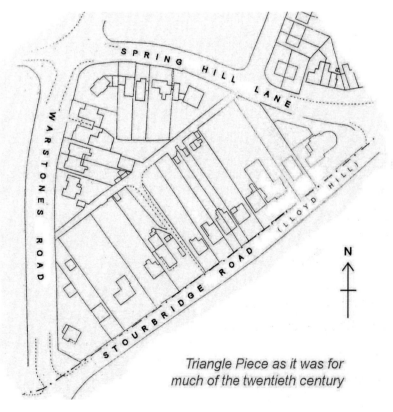

Triangle Piece as it was for much of the twentieth century

We know that Rose Cottage was the first property to be built in this portion of Springhill Lane, the date probably being 1918. Argyll was built in 1922 and Virginia Cottage (The Cottage) by 1924.

The two largest plots in the Triangle were developed as garages/petrol stations. Post First World War motor vehicle numbers increased tremendously. There was a surplus of ex-army lorries available for those wishing to build their own transport companies and many were converted to buses. Added to this Wolverhampton was a centre of production for motorcars, motorcycles, buses and lorries and this in its turn led to the establishment of garages on our arterial roads. By the 1930s Penn had four or five of them on Lloyd Hill/Penn Rd and one on the Warstones Road. The best sites were those at the top of Lloyd Hill, then a single-track road where vehicles had to labour up the steep and continuous slope from Wombourne. Having changed down gear several times drivers were travelling at a slow pace and could easily pull onto the station forecourts.

Boulton's garage – the sign was made from part of the tail of an S.E.5 biplane

HW Boulton's 'Penn Nib' motorcycle

A man who could see both the dawning of the motorcar age and the possibilities that a garage on Lloyd Hill presented was Herbert William Boulton – 'Bertie' and sometimes 'Bill' to his friends.

He had opened his first refuelling station at the bottom of Church Hill in 1919, where he sold petrol in two-gallon cans. His second outlet was his garage on the Stourbridge Road, which is currently portrayed by empty

50

ground that lies underdeveloped. One of his advertising signs had been adapted from the tailplane of an S.E.5 biplane, an RAF fighter aircraft of the First World War. Here he sold BP and Pratts petrol. Here too Bertie built several motorcycles, both two- and four-stroke, naming them the Penn Nib with the petrol tank in this form.

Motorcyclists used the garage as an unofficial meeting point and when the local sergeant and police constable were not about the bikers ran their own time trials. Machines and riders were lined up across Lloyd Hill, racing off to the Rose and Crown before ascending Church Hill, negotiating the twin hairpins at the Church and at the Stag, before accelerating down the Common. The gruelling climb up to Gospel End was a real test for man and machine, whilst the difficult descent to the Wodehouse Island demanded total concentration. The long slow climb up Lloyd Hill was the last part of the 'TT' course, a stopwatch being pressed as they passed Lloyd Hill garage!

Bertie had negotiated a contract with the Ford Motor Company who imported their cars through Manchester docks. Those which were driven to showrooms in the south called in at Lloyd Hill to refuel. The Boultons lived on site in their bungalow. Bertie took a job as a motorcycle tester in 1925 at the AJS and sold his garage. He made little from his stock.

By the mid-1920s Jack Read, who had been the manager, bought the plot and developed it. Eventually the bungalow's front was redesigned and a similar one built to match it on the other side of the plot. Between them were the doors leading to the workshops and the parking lot which led to the back lane. J Read and Sons continued trading until the 1970s, for most of the time selling Esso products and only latterly VIP petrol. Heron holdings then ran the site for petrol sales, selling Fina petrol products.

Two doors up Mr Grafton opened the Terminus Garage. At first he lived in a coach with a lean-to shop alongside. Mr Groves followed him, selling Wolverhampton Corporation the land in 1927 for a turning circle for their motorbuses. The Penn route had been extended in this year from the Rose and Crown to Springhill to meet the demands of a fast urbanising Upper Penn. Trolleybuses followed in 1935. Subsequently the house, shop and the art deco garage and showroom were built, trading until the 1960s. Each evening the night air was lit by the pump globes of the Shell, BP, Power, National Benzole and Dominion fuels, attracting the passing motorists' attention. Only the petrol sales have gone, for the Cooperative store has re-established Groves' grocery business and meets local demand. A separate car service centre uses part of the 1930s garage and a tile business also operates from the site.

Triangle Piece's land use continues to change. The back lane separating the properties facing the Stourbridge Road and those facing Springhill Lane is no longer a through byway and Reads' Garage and the neighbouring demolished house sites await further development. Many of the properties fronting the Stourbridge Road have been rebuilt and redeveloped and it is a far cry from the sheep pasture of 1843 and 1901.

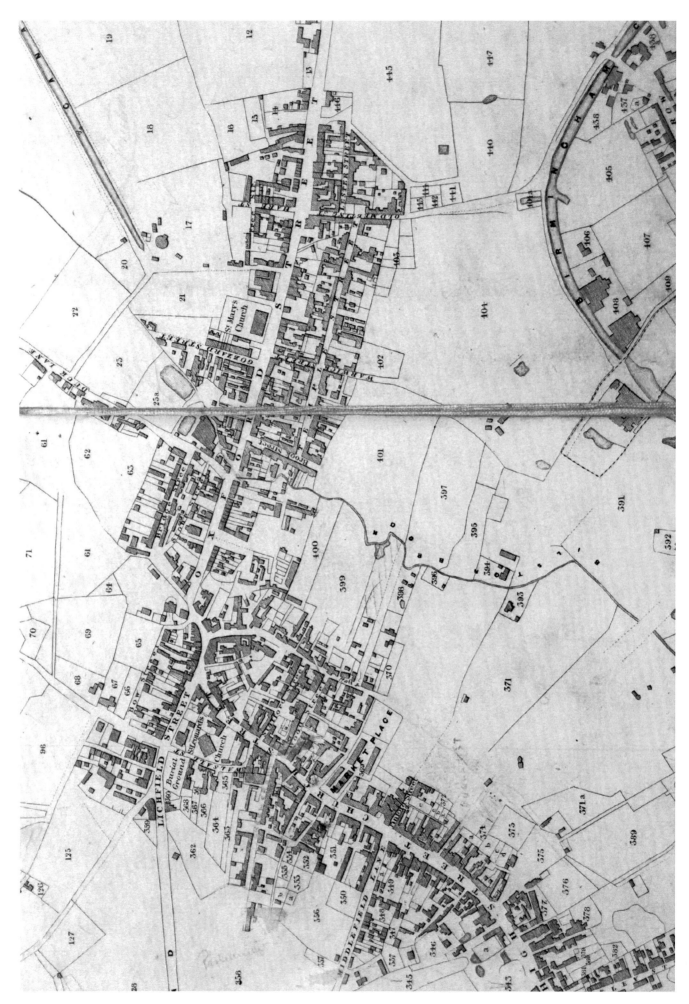

52

There has been much criticism about the lack of urgency and the uncoordinated approach by the international community in helping West African states tackle ebola. Fortunately there is now more aid and a stronger co-ordination of measures to tackle the disease and these are slowly having an impact. Currently nearly 7000 people have died! The world could have learnt much from an event that affected the people of the Black Country, and particularly of Bilston some 180 years ago.

In 1832 a cholera epidemic hit Britain and communities waited to see if they would be spared. The well–to-do people of nearby Bilston, an industrial township of coal mines, ironworks, manufactories and stone quarries, held a meeting to see if they needed to set up a local Board of Health to deal with the impending threat. They decided that there was no need at that time (March 1832). They believed Bilston's problem lay in the lack of morals displayed by the lower classes, rather than in the lack of properly sewered housing and a clean water supply. They failed to understand that disease was most prevalent in the very worst parts of their township. The Reverend Leigh, incumbent of St Leonard's, the parish church, commented that Bilston was set on rising ground and the Bilston Brook, which flowed through the township, had never caused a problem. Nevertheless, they decided to keep a watching brief, especially when the cholera reached Tipton.

In those days the cause of cholera was little understood, even by prominent medical men and perhaps their decision was more about keeping the poor rate down than reducing possible risk. This initial inertia was to cost them dear.

The 29th July saw the start of the annual, and much looked forward to Bilston Wakes Week. It began with large Sunday Church and Chapel services where the collections helped pay for the annual Sunday School programmes. These were followed by parades and much feasting and drinking. The Wake was not cancelled as it would be nowadays.

It is of no surprise to learn that on 4th August, Mr Proctor, one of the doctors working in Bilston called upon the Reverend Leigh to inform him that the cholera had reached Bilston. Elizabeth Dawson, aged 35, of Temple Street; Richard Dyke, aged 16, of Bridge Street; and Mary Cleaton, aged 2, of Hall Street, had all been struck down. They all lived with 400 yards of each other in poor homes, within 200 yards of the Bilston Brook.

It was at this point that the Reverend Leigh acted swiftly and took charge. A Board of Health was appointed and retrospective approval sought from London. It met each day and was made up of the churchwardens of St Leonard's (John Etheridge was later remembered for his selfless work by the naming of a school after him), medical men and the leading citizens of the town.

They staffed the hospital by appointing additional doctors, students and nurses, opened a free dispensary, arranged transport for those needing hospitalisation, provided for the removal of bodies and free burial, made lime available at no charge to householders so that they could lime-wash their houses, and arranged for the disinfecting of properties where householders had died of cholera. As St Leonard's burial ground was almost full St Mary's and the Wesleyan Methodists made their grounds available. The clergy worked together for the good of the townspeople. To avoid the spread of the disease Sunday services were cancelled at St Leonard's and family and friends discouraged from attending the grave, which in many cases was a burial pit.

As the number of deaths rose and as the township ground to a standstill the Reverend Leigh appealed to Central Government and the nation as a whole for help. Dr McCann was despatched from London to take charge of medical matters. He stopped the mixing of hospital patients with those in the poor house next door.

The following figures are an indicator of how dire the situation was:

Period	Cases	Deaths	Approx Ratio
4-10 August	150	36	1 in 4
11-17 August	616	133	1 in 4.5
18-24 August	924	298	1 in 3
25-31 August	832	184	1 in 4.5
1-7 September	694	62	1 in 11
8-14 September	250	23	1 in 11
15-21 September	102	6	1 in 17
Totals	3568	742	1 in 5

The Reverend Leigh was responsible for appealing for help from the nation in Bilston's hour of need. The response can only be described as terrific as £8536-8-7d was raised, and spent, in supporting Bilstonians. Fashionable towns like Bath, Brighton and Cheltenham; major industrial centres like Birmingham, Newcastle under Lyme, Blackburn and Stoke; market towns such as Bridgnorth, Stone, Crickhowell and Church Stretton; cathedral cities like Hereford; sister Black Country townships such as West Bromwich and Sedgley (which also suffered); and nearby villages such as Codsall, Tettenhall and Claverley; all came to Bilston's aid.

The congregations of churches and chapels, some far off, contributed and within these were many "widows' mites". Adelaide, the wife of King William IV contributed as did her rival the Duchess of Kent (the future Queen Victoria's mother), and the nobility followed suit. A dozen or so Earls, including those of Dudley, Dartmouth and Stamford and Warrington, and Sir John Wrottesley, Bart., MP were among the subscribers to Bilston's relief. High profile clergy made their contribution as was the case with the Bishop of Lichfield and Coventry and the Dean of Wolverhampton.

Penn was not left out. Squire William Bradney Pershouse of Penn Hall and Mrs Pershouse both made donations. The Reverend William Dalton of the Lloyd and the Reverend Thursby, Vicar of Penn, as well as his family, took up Bilston's plight. Other local benefactors included TWH Grazebrook of Dallicott; W Herrick of Merridale House (Bantock House); Henry Jesson of Trysull Manor; Thomas Peach Pudsey and John Aston, both of Seisdon; and Mary Tongue of Orton.

The seven weeks of hell that Bilston endured resulted in the loss of 1 in 20 of its inhabitants; 131 widows lost their breadwinner; 103 widowers lost their wives; 198 orphans lost their mother; and 199 orphans lost their father. Sedgley with a population of 20,577 lost 290 to cholera, Darlaston with 6667 inhabitants lost 68 and Wolverhampton with 30,600 just 193. At its worst, in a seven day period Bilston lost 309 of its people.

The best of human nature was seen. Two Bilston doctors gave their lives by working with cholera victims. Dr McCann, sent from the central board of Health in London worked tirelessly in trying to combat the disease and the Reverend Leigh and his local board gave all their energies to organising support for the ill and their families. One of Leigh's churchwarden's is still remembered by an older generation who learnt of his good work from the oral history tradition, passed down from family member to family member across the generations. John Etheridge had prior to 1832 worked to improve the lot of the poor. He set up Sunday schools and taught miners to read; paid for and distributed bibles and set up a savings bank and a clothing club. After the epidemic had passed the cholera school was set up for the orphans of 1832 and he superintended this. He organised the distribution of funds raised for the cholera victims. Again in the 1849 cholera outbreak he worked tirelessly for Bilstonians.

Supplying the poor with bread	£296-7-11d
Supplying the poor with mutton	£511-5-6
Supplying the poor with oatmeal	£15-1-4
Supplying widows and orphans with money	£982-1-4
Supplying bedding and clothing	£898-15-8
Providing servant and other expenses for distribution of above	£60-12-11
Providing lime	£25-8-4
Presented to the Board of Health towards defraying expenses of the hospital and those receiving at the dispensary	£500-0-0
Providing stationery	£45-6-8
Advertising for contributions	£43-3-6
Paying for the erection of a school for cholera orphans	£400-0-0
Lent on mortgage on real security the interest to be applied In paying for salaries of a master and mistress	£2000-0-0
Purchase of £2000 of exchange bills to enable committee to continue weekly allowances to necessitous widows and orphans by cholera	£2030-15-0
In Bankers' hands this 7th April 1833	£266-6-0
Total	£8536-8-7d

Leigh and his board kept records of all donations and published the accounts of how it had been spent. They not only put in place structures to cope with the epidemic, but also arranged for those made destitute to receive food and clothing. Further they planned for a post-cholera Bilston as the accounts show (above on page 55).

After the event a fund was set up to provide a place of Anglican worship at Catchems Corner at Ettingshall. £3000 was required and by the 7th April 1833 £1041-8-0 had been promised and £572-2-0 paid into the fund. The first stone was laid by Lord Ward on May 30th, 1834. The architect was Robert Ebbels. It was opened for divine service on 4th September, 1835 and consecrated on 23rd August, 1837. It could seat 928 and served a very populous district.

Dr McCann in his final report did not say that Bilston's unclean water was to blame. Like others in the township they had concentrated their energies on dealing with the epidemic as best as they could. McCann's main finding was that where cholera occurred there was a need to set up a free dispensary, which could prescribe for peoples' bowel complaints. Medical science had failed to establish that cholera is spread through infected water and food and lack of hygiene.

1832 passed and the threat of cholera was forgotten, only to revisit in 1848/9, when hundreds again fell victim in Bilston. The absence of effective local government could be potentially tackled with the 1835 Municipal Corporations Act, which provided for the election of town councils every three years by male ratepayers. These were the very class keeping the poor rate down, so poor housing and bad water supply continued. It was left to National Government to legislate in 1848 with a public health act, but a locality did not have to have a local health board unless mortality was high. Another 30 years was to pass before Disraeli's Government passed the Artisans' Dwelling Act which permitted, but did not force councils to clear slum districts. However, this does not detract from the evidence that the very best of human nature was displayed by wide sections of the British public in their attempt to help their fellow citizens in industrial Bilston, a Black Country township of some 14,492 inhabitants.

The 1832 experience in Bilston reminds us that strong, effective and caring leadership, which sought the support of the community and which not only dealt with the difficult issues during the epidemic, but planned for the peoples' future, allowed for the best possible outcomes, from what had been a dire situation. The Reverend Leigh and his committee are an example to us all.

Our medieval forebears knew the qualities of the sparrowhawk and its ability to provide a ready meal for the lord of the manor's table. Partridge, quail, rabbit, hare and woodpigeon were all at danger from this bird. In 1200 Adam de Dunstanville, lord of the manor of Shifnal, exempted his vassal, Olim, from all taxes and tolls if he trained a sparrowhawk at his own expense for his lord. The bird's importance was again demonstrated in 1259 when a keeper of eyries of sparrowhawks was appointed for the extensive Cannock forest.

My son was, and still is, very active. He played for his primary school football team from the age of 7 and represented Staffordshire at cricket at under-11 before we left the district for South Glamorgan. He played cricket for this county as a schoolboy, going on tour to Malaysia and Singapore at under-18 level.

We had a large garden in Showell Lane. He would practice his ball skills on the top lawn, which was of tennis court size. A long garage lay on the plot boundary, with glazed metal door leading via steps onto the lawn beneath. A gazebo effect was created by a privet hedge on one side of the path and mature beech, larch and sycamore trees on the other side. The more I warned my son of the dangers of kicking the football towards the house and garage, the more he seemed to prove his accuracy. Two re-glazes to the door panels later I had had enough and I became determined to put in specially strengthened and thickened glass, which would withstand a misdirected football.

A regular visitor to the garden was an attractive male sparrowhawk. At about 13 inches long with his blue-grey back, orange chest and rufous underparts barred with brown, he cut a dash in more senses than one. As both my neighbour, whose backdoor opened onto the privet hedge, and myself fed our garden birds throughout the year we always had sparrows, finches, thrushes, blackbirds and robins aplenty to watch and enjoy.

The sparrowhawk was well suited to the Penn countryside with its woodland, copse, open field and garden landscapes. It liked to nest high in a conifer, preferably a larch. Often it took over a disused nest of a carrion crow, magpie or even on occasion a woodpigeon's meagre platform. It was not averse to driving out a grey squirrel from its dray. On one of these bases it built its nest – an untidy array of twigs and sticks, the cup of which was lined with fir-bark chippings and down. The female, the larger bird and clothed in brown with barred underparts, would incubate the single clutch of 4 to 6 rounded bluish or greenish white eggs which were blotched with red and brown. The male's role was quite clearly to feed both its partner and the hatchlings and it therefore had to work extremely hard to supply ten or so small birds a day. Where it had taken a large bird it would stop off at a favourite perch to remove the feathers and divide the carcass before handing it over to the female bird. Outside the nesting season the female will take even larger birds such as woodpigeon, jays, pheasants and even farmyard hens. Strangely for most of the year the male and female birds live apart.

In flight the sparrowhawk's short rounded wings and long tail allow it to accurately negotiate woodland corridors at rapid speed over short distances. The bird is a raider, an ambusher and an inflictor of terror on garden birds. At our old garden it would regularly hunt both sides of the privet corridor with success; flying low and skimming the surface before taking its chosen victim in flight. It is a spirited and daring bird with a reckless determination, which I liked to think its bright yellow eyes represented.

On one fateful day just as he was finishing off his attack on the sparrows on the hedge, my neighbour unknowingly opened her back door. The sparrowhawk startled, broke off its attack and flew into what he thought was our open garage space. His way was barred by the heavy duty glass of the door and tragically he fell to the ground with a broken neck.

We felt great sadness at his loss, the more so as his brood was now without the breadwinner. This species suffered in the 1950s and 1960s from agricultural spraying of crops with toxic pesticides. Once these were banned the number of sparrowhawks was slowly recovering so this additional loss was painful. Rather than place the body in the bin an ornithologist friend of mine requested that I place the dead bird in the deep freeze, until his next visit from Essex. Normally he would never have sought out a taxidermist, but the prowess of this south Staffordshire sparrowhawk lives on as an exhibit.

The whole experience of the bird's recklessness, my son's sporting enthusiasm, my re-glazing with toughened glass, my neighbour opening her door at the wrong moment and my failure to use stickers on the glass to warn birds off all led to the law of unintended consequences. Hopefully a sequence of events not to be repeated!

Farm cottages & central office (top)

Cowhouses for 40, northern range (middle left)

Stable block cottage (above)

Bricked-up cartsheds, southern range (left)

A cousin of mine spent more than twenty years searching for the right kind of eighteenth or nineteenth century barn to come on the market so that he could convert it into a twenty-first century home. In the event he found it just over the Shropshire border and tastefully restored it with oak flooring and surfaces, keeping the rich red hue of the brickwork. Many have done the same, thus retaining for the benefit of all, the rural scene that was once so common amongst our lanes and byways. Nevertheless, we have lost many farmyard buildings as they have ceased to meet modern farming needs. Bearnett farmhouse and barns were flattened as the farm became part of a larger unit; Orton Grange lost some of its barns as it was cheaper to pull them down than repair them; Lloyd Farm's Georgian farmhouse went under the dual carriageway; whilst many of Trescott Grange's farm buildings fell into disrepair, to give but four examples.

It is therefore unusual to find a farm that has continued to maintain its very extensive buildings and yards, without selling them off. I recently visited one such place. Until the twentieth century most of South Staffordshire's farms were owned by large estates. Over the first seventy years of the twentieth century many of these were broken up and the farms bought by sitting tenants or others wishing to try their hand at making the land pay. The Penn Hall estate was sold in 1899; The Lloyd in 1901; The Duke of Sutherland's Penn Estates in 1917; and Bearnett in 1924. The great estates of Lord Wrottesley were auctioned off in 1929 and in 1963, those of the Earl of Dudley in 1947. The Earl of Dartmouth's influence at Patshull Hall ceased when it was used as a rehabilitation centre during the war years, and afterwards as an occupational therapy centre for the local hospital trust, before being sold off and running as a wedding venue.

The farm I visited was once one of these estate farms and it played a pivotal role beyond its own boundaries with the estate bailiff living there and managing the estate's affairs from his office in the yard. This farm's buildings lie to the immediate east of the modern farmhouse, which has art nouveau features. They are very extensive and are arranged in an east-west figure of eight with an additional smaller yard to the south. On entry to the very large first yard two cottages lie on the right and the former boiler house, dairy and sterilising room on the left. In the entrance once stood the stand for the milk churns, which were collected daily by lorry. Along the upper side of the yard are cowhouses for 40, whilst opposite are a saddle room and stables. The stables have been converted into a cottage. Beyond is the entrance to the third yard, whilst the southern range is completed by bricked up cartsheds which open out into this smaller third farmyard. In the middle of the large yard is the quaint red brick farm office and traces of a range of piggeries, which would have approached the buildings of the southern range. The fourth side of the yard is made up of a huge red brick and tiled traditional South Staffordshire barn. In the middle of the barn is a 'driftway', which stretches from the ground to the roof, so as to allow the load carried by the tallest harvest wain to pass unhindered. On the first floor to the right is the granary, with outside steps and a throughway beneath, allowing access to the rickyard beyond when the driftway is blocked by wagons; whilst to the left reached by its own staircase is the storage area.

Coachhouse, small yard (above)

Granary steps with throughway under (right)

The driftway, looking from the east (below) and from the west (bottom right)

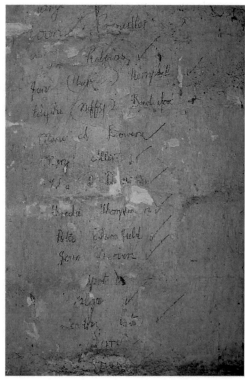

Signatures of German PoWs (top left)
and of land girls (top right) on wall in workshop

Pregnant sow in bullpen (left)

Scarecrow, modern barn (below left)

Pigeon holes in driftway barn
where kestrels nest (below)

Beyond is an extensive second yard, originally and still the rickyard. Up against the driftway barn is the workshop in which are the signatures of the land girls and the German prisoners of war who worked these lands in the early and mid 1940s. In the rickyard the buildings have been largely re-roofed and rebuilt and provide cover for the machinery, hay and straw and livestock. Two Dutch barns have been replaced with modern clear span barns.

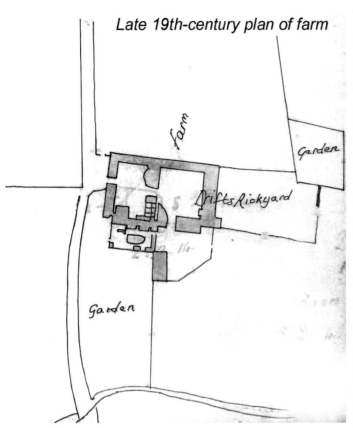

Late 19th-century plan of farm

The farmyard scene is completed by the smaller third yard, which includes a livestock yard and a range of bullpens. These are currently in use by sows. The former coach house is part of this range. The curved walls of the former stable block and the fold yard wall on the opposite corner of the yard, evidence the skill of the original bricklayers and the purpose of such structures – to avoid injury to the cattle as they push and jostle each other for entry and exit.

The property included two brick labourers' cottages near to the farmhouse and two on the edge of a wood. The latter were sold off as surplus to modern requirements. They once contained scullery, living room, pantry and two bedrooms. Those nearest to the farmhouse are much as they were in the 19th century, with black lead grates and cool cellars, where milk, cheese, hams and rough cider/small beer would be stored. These cottages had an extremely large vegetable and garden plot running down to the brook, whilst the farmhouse's garden lay north east of the rickyard. Self-sufficiency in all things was the aim of every nineteenth-century farm. When the snow is down and it has begun to thaw or when there is a period of drought and the grass begins to turn yellow a secret is revealed, for a circular outline appears four yards from the cottages' wall – this marks the site of the farm well. It may well have been fed by the watercourse which runs underground from the north side of the yard, or it could be a well into the sandstone aquifer itself.

The land has been highly cultivated despite its very varied soils. These consist of free draining fluvio-glacial deposits laid down in and after the last ice age; soils which overlie sandstones; a relatively small area of pebble bed derived soils; and the red clays and marls of the Upper and Middle Coal Measures.

Whilst one might have expected the farm's underlying geology to

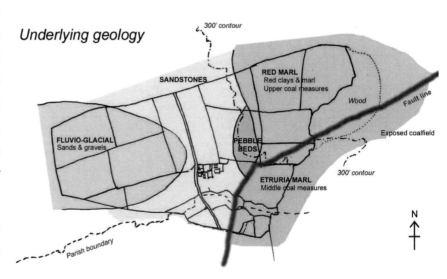

Underlying geology

66

determine land use, this has not always been the case. It is economic considerations that have been responsible for the colours displayed in the landscape each summer and autumn. In 1947 some 68% of the farm's land was down to arable as Britain tried to feed as much of its population as possible. Government policy in a broken post war Britain was to restrict imports and expand exports in an attempt to meet its balance of payments deficit and to begin to repay the huge debts the country had accrued throughout the War Years. As a result farmers were given attractive subsidies to produce food. Some 25% was down to pasture and the remaining 7% was taken up with such things as watercourses and roads.

One hundred years earlier at the time of the tythe survey in 1841 the arable acreage was an even greater proportion (77%) of the farm; with only 18% down to pasture and 5% for other uses (osier

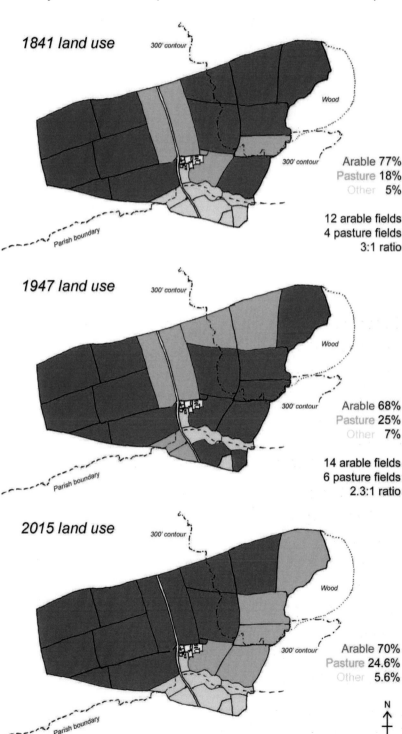

1841 land use

Arable 77%
Pasture 18%
Other 5%

12 arable fields
4 pasture fields
3:1 ratio

1947 land use

Arable 68%
Pasture 25%
Other 7%

14 arable fields
6 pasture fields
2.3:1 ratio

2015 land use

Arable 70%
Pasture 24.6%
Other 5.6%

beds, woodland, watercourses, and roads). The tythe was originally a tenth payment on the produce of the land. The Tithe Commutation Act of 1836 substituted a monetary payment and detailed maps for each parish were drawn up, showing who held the land, the land use and the tythe payable.

The land use percentages are explained by the government policy of the period. This enforced a rigid protectionism with regard to British farming, its aim to make Britain self-sufficient in food production by giving landowners and tenant farmers a worthwhile economic return for their labours. During the French and Napoleonic Wars of the late 18th and early 19th century this policy paid off. But, as Britain continued to industrialise and as its population grew an increase in the amount of imported food was essential, if sections of the population were not to starve and if bread riots were to be avoided. Various price mechanisms and price thresholds were employed to try and manage the situation. However, despite the introduction of better farming methods from the 1750s onwards, which gave higher crop yields and more valuable and productive livestock there were many who advocated a free trade approach. It was argued that this would greatly assist Britain in selling its manufactured goods across the world, whilst allowing food imports to feed its growing population. The land use percentages given reflect the situation before the Repeal of the Corn Laws in 1846. After repeal world markets were more open. In the event, the period 1846-1875 did not see farming lose out as prices remained reasonably stable, given that there were peaks and troughs in the harvests. It was only when New World cereals and meat became readily available in the last quarter of the nineteenth century that British farming entered the doldrums.

Today, this farm rears 25-30 beef cattle and 15 sows and followers. As manufactured animal feed is expensive 70% of the land is down to arable, the crops being grown for animal feed (oil seed rape, beans and barley). The surplus feedstuffs are sold on. A further 24.6% of land is down to pasture, whilst 5.6% is for other uses (roadways, wood, pools and waste). It can be seen that land use has not changed considerably over the last 175 years and that farmers have reacted to market needs.

Neither have field names altered much. There is still a Gravel Pit field, so named because gravel has been extracted from the pebble beds. There is also a field called Pikes, quite a common name on farms as it reflects the shape of the field – a narrow pointed piece of land at the side of a field of irregular shape. Other field names are also descriptive as in the case of Brick Kiln Piece referring to the clay taken to produce the bricks for early farm buildings; Mer Clay which might mean marl/clay; Bates Orchard suggesting a former tenant farmer; and Flax Pits. Here a small pool lies at its edge. Flax was grown in this district over many centuries. It was then placed in pools and watercourses, so that the inner stalk could be 'retted' or rotted away, leaving the outer fibres intact. These were beaten in the fulling mill by stamps and turned into twine or coarse linen. A rivulet flows westwards from the pool and also drains these red clays.

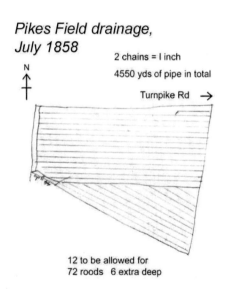

Pikes Field drainage, July 1858

2 chains = I inch

4550 yds of pipe in total

Turnpike Rd →

N

12 to be allowed for
72 roods   6 extra deep

Gravel Pit Piece field drainage, January 1860

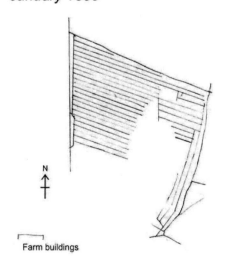

N

Farm buildings

This farm has some mid nineteenth century drainage maps. At a time when labour was cheap and plentiful they give witness to the huge amount of manual toil in laying these drains. The drains are in the main of an early design – a flat base on top of which was placed a porous oval shaped section. In Pikes field alone an amazing 4550 yards of pipe was laid at a depth of some 4 to 5 feet. The Gravel Pit Piece map shows that the

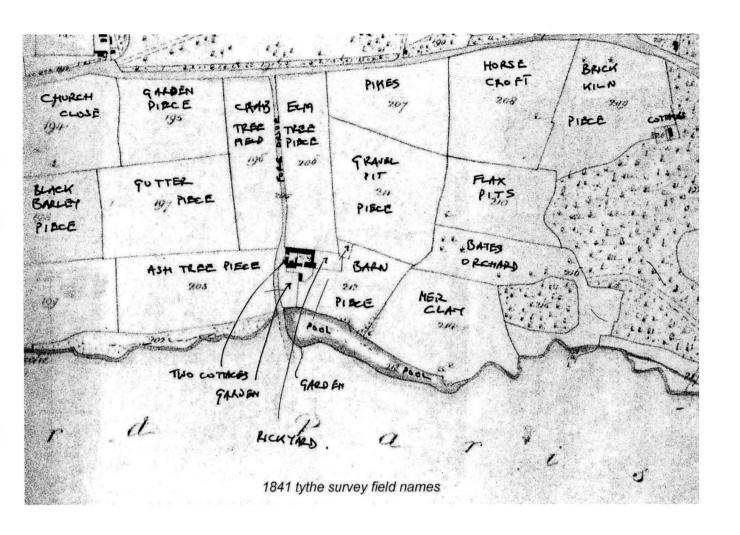

CHURCH CLOSE 194

GARDEN PIECE 195

CRAB TREE FIELD 196

ELM TREE PIECE 206

PIKES 207

HORSE CROFT 268

BRICK KILN PIECE 209

COTTAGE

BLACK BARLEY PIECE

GUTTER PIECE 197

GRAVEL PIT 211 PIECE

FLAX PITS 210

ASH TREE PIECE 203

BARN 212 PIECE

BATES ORCHARD 216

MER CLAY 214

POOL

TWO COTTAGES GARDEN

GARDEN

POOL

RICKYARD.

r   d   P   a   r   i   s

1841 tythe survey field names

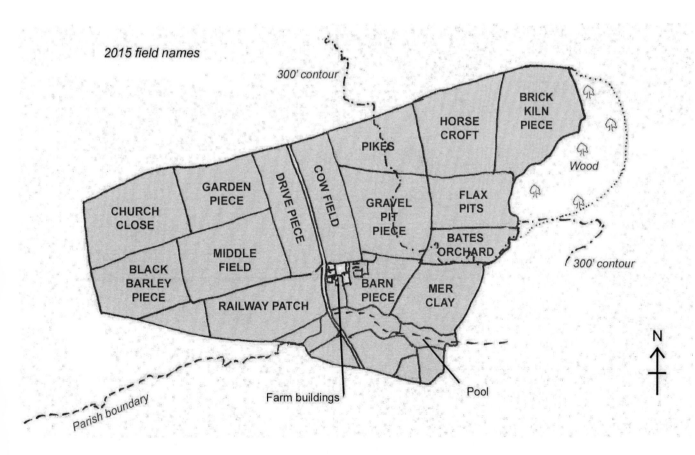

2015 field names

300' contour

BRICK KILN PIECE

PIKES

HORSE CROFT

Wood

GARDEN PIECE

DRIVE PIECE

COW FIELD

GRAVEL PIT PIECE

FLAX PITS

CHURCH CLOSE

MIDDLE FIELD

BATES ORCHARD

300' contour

BLACK BARLEY PIECE

BARN PIECE

MER CLAY

RAILWAY PATCH

Pool

Farm buildings

Parish boundary

N

GWR landslip, July 1915

farmer knew exactly where clay occurred and laid on drainage accordingly.

Field size and layout is very similar to that of past centuries. Some land has been lost to railway construction, but in the main this has been on the edge of the steep river valley. Ash Tree Piece has been renamed Railway Patch, but hedgerow ash trees are still very much in evidence. One or two fields have been joined either by removal of hedges or by leaving access points for stock to roam. The GWR railway constructed a high embankment to carry its rails across the marshy valley, the stream being culverted and brick abutments built to protect the channel. These were in place by March of 1915, but the contractors suffered a setback in July of that year, when heavy rains and flooding caused a slip which left the rails unsupported. A further set back was that men and materials became increasingly scarce as the demands of war engulfed Europe. It was left to the post war years to complete the line, a link between Wolverhampton and Stourbridge, and a by-pass to the congested lines of the Black Country. It did not open until 1925.

The valley was also affected by a private mineral railway, as well as by spoil from coal and clay mining. It cut the header pond for the local mill in two which resulted in it silting up. The powerful stream which falls off the South Staffordshire plateau had driven many corn mills and forges along its course, but corn milling began to succumb from the 1880s and by the 1920s it was finished in this valley. The osier beds were also affected. They had been cultivated for their willows, which were used in basket making and the making of hurdles, or sheep fences. The track from the south accesses the farm via a bridge over the brook. The bridge has been constructed to allow water to

flow through at three different levels. Presumably this was a device to regulate water supply for the mill downstream and/or to get rid of excess flows from the pool upstream.

With the silting up of the pool a new habitat resulted for wetland birds and insects, and species not seen here before set up home. Another resident of this farm is the lapwing. When cultivating the farmers

Silted-up pool

are careful to avoid its nests – a scrape in the earth with a bit of grass thrown in for good measure. Four or five olive or dark buff elongated eggs are laid, the tapered end pointing inwards to the nest's centre, thereby providing protection against wind. Both eggs and young hatchlings are difficult to see because of their colour; they look just like stones, as the young birds freeze if they are approached. The lapwing populations have been seriously reduced and doubtless there are a number of reasons for this. As the fox and buzzard numbers have increased fewer eggs and chicks have survived. These days the farm is lucky to have two nests on its lands. Each spring kestrels nest in the pigeon holes in one of the barns, whilst some 15 or so pairs of swallows make their homes in the sheds.

Lapwing

A strong visual feature is a field bank, which demarcates the boundary of the exposed coalfield. Here the Etruria Marls of the Upper Coal Measures are downthrown under the Triassic sandstones. However the most striking feature is the very nearly complete set of farmyard ranges that the surprised visitor is confronted with. It is to the credit of the owners that they have managed to adapt, whilst still retaining a scene which the 1840s tenant farmer, the estate bailiff of the early 1900s and the Second World War land girls and prisoners of war would recognise.

The faultline between Mer Clay and Barn fields

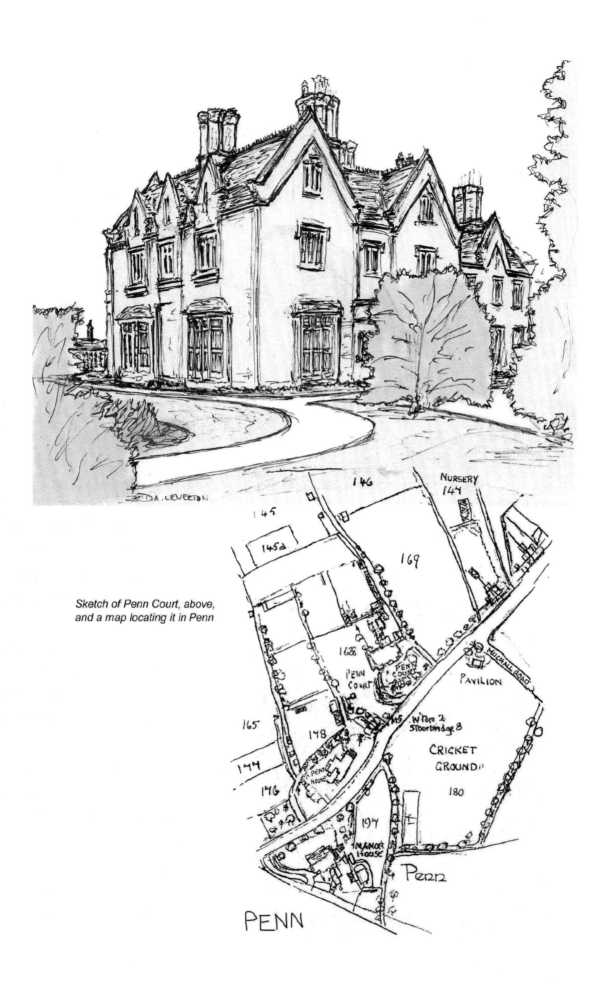

Sketch of Penn Court, above, and a map locating it in Penn

72

By 1835 Penn had begun to see an influx of wealthy families as they moved away from the smoke and unsanitary conditions of a fast-expanding manufacturing town. The fields at the bottom of Graiseley Hill would remain in part for a little longer, but nothing would stop the engulfing nature of Wolverhampton. Pigot in his Staffordshire directory of that year could report that "the village of Penn, which is situated about 2 miles south west from Wolverhampton is principally inhabited by respectable families connected with that town".

Penn had always had a few notable families who were blessed with land and imposing houses. There were the Bradney/Pershouses of Penn Hall and the Marshes at Lloyd House, and then there were the Thackers, solicitors at Georgian Muchall Hall. The Victorian age would see many more, but this time they were merchant capitalists and captains of industry. They bought up several acres and built their fine residences along Penn Road from Graiseley Hill to Earlswood and Bearnett on Lloyd Hill. Pigot mentions Joseph Pearson at Graisley House, later to become the site of the AJS motorcycle works. The Hollies, Hillside, The Mount, Oaklands and Claremont were nearby. A little further out Goldthorn Hill was a favoured site. Beyond were Bromley House, Muchall Grove, The Uplands, Penn Court, Pennhouse, Penn Manor, The Woodlands (replacing Penn Villa), Pencroft and Foxlands.

Penn Court and grounds, like many of the above residences, went for residential development. Today Osborne Road covers its site. It was the home of William Hanbury Sparrow, a prudent businessman and very wealthy ironmaster. In 1844 he owned 12 acres in Penn and bought the house from John Underhill, another ironmaster, who then lived at Goldthorn Hill House. The Sparrows had come from Audley in north Staffordshire about the year 1750, attracted by opportunities in the south Staffordshire coal and iron industries. A descendant, William Sparrow of Pattingham was born 1st March 1764 and married Mary, the daughter of Thomas Hanbury of Birmingham. From this union William Hanbury Sparrow was conceived. He was born in 1789.

Along with John William Sparrow, who later resided at Beckminster House, he was a member of the firm of W and JS Sparrow. They owned Bilston mill, where rods, bars and hoops of good quality were made. They also owned Stowheath furnaces. It was reported that William Hanbury was worth £1.5 million.

Although extremely wealthy, William Hanbury Sparrow was described as "respected, cautious, plain in manner, discrete and having a bundle of common sense". Like many nineteenth-century entrepreneurs he took his duties seriously and displayed a genuine paternalism for his fellow workers.

By the 1850s Penn needed a second church. In 1849 he had purchased additional land from the Duke of Sutherland's estate, which allowed him to give the land on which St Philip's was built. William

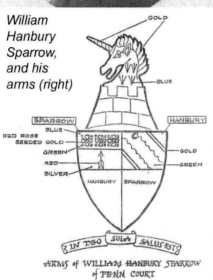

William Hanbury Sparrow, and his arms (right)

ARMS of WILLIAM HANBURY SPARROW
of PENN COURT

was the main contributor to the building fund, also giving the organ and the west window with its four lights. He laid the foundation stone on 15th May, 1858 and was presented with an inscribed silver trowel by the architect, Mr Griffin.

In Bilston William was responsible for setting up the Bilston District Banking Company, which prospered and became one of the best managed banks in the district. He died in 1867, loved and mourned by the many across the social divides. Unlike Penn Court his memory lives on in the beautiful east window at St Bartholomew's church. If you are there as the winter sun awakens, a feast of colour is set free, filling the chancel with an amazing light. This richness is also to be found in the words painted onto the glass: *'Peace be still'; 'I am with you always'; 'Lord save me'; 'The Word was made flesh'; 'I am the good shepherd'.* The inscription at the base reads, *'To the Glory of God and in memory of William Hanbury Sparrow'*, and was placed by his daughters Emma and Harriette. Harriette also gave St Bart's its brass lecturn.

After William Hanbury's death his son William Mander Sparrow lived at Penn Court, and after his death his sister Mrs Emma Fowke. Emma had married Thomas Henry Fowke, a surgeon at The Staffordshire General Infirmary (The Royal) in 1846. They first of all lived on Graisley Hill. She died in 1896 and is buried in the churchyard at St Bartholomew's.

For a brief time a Mr Emmonds was the occupier of the Court, before the house was sold to a member of another important family of ironmasters. 1902 was probably the first year that Victor Emmanuel Hickman and his family were in residence. The house and grounds were described in a book on Staffordshire Leaders of 1907 as "charming and one of the chief seats in the busy industrial area of Wolverhampton". Penn Court was certainly a suitable residence for a man of social, commercial and financial standing.

Victor had been born in 1863 and his father's choice of names suggests that he admired Victor Emmanuel, who as a figurehead saw Italy united in 1861. Victor was educated at Cambridge, graduating in 1884. He married Ethel Margaret, the daughter of Edward Brown Fitton of

Victor Emmanuel Hickman

Fair Lea, Great Malvern in 1889. Victor, the sixth son of Sir Alfred Hickman, Bt., was a director of the family firm based at Springvale which had strong and successful interests in iron, steel and coal.

Victor supported Joseph Chamberlain's fiscal policy of ending free trade, protecting the iron trade from European imports and giving Empire preference to materials and foodstuffs. At the same time

he was a kind and generous employer and was a popular country gentleman. He took his responsibilities seriously, being a JP (from 1905), a governor of the Royal Orphanage and a member of the board of the Wolverhampton and Staffordshire General hospital. His son and heir was Commander Geoffrey Victor Hickman RN, who was born in 1890.

Life at Penn Court in the early years of the twentieth century was one of privilege and pleasure. Servants met the domestic needs and kept the house and gardens in excellent order. The family's social calendar was built around meeting up with the social set and followed the seasons. A typical programme included riding to hounds with the Albrighton Hunt in winter, skiing and tobogganing at Celerina, Switzerland, Eights week at Oxford for trying out punting on the Isis, and summer was reserved for weekends at the cottage at Hatfield or visiting friends in a variety of houses such as Tandridge Hall (Surrey), Wyastone Leys (near Monmouth), Portsdown Lodge (Hampshire) and Glynn Park and Castle Dobbs in northern Ireland. It was still fashionable to stay at Scarborough for a seaside holiday, whilst a sojourn at Llandrindod Wells to take the waters completed the season. Nearer to home agricultural shows were visited, whilst the children took part in the Albrighton Hunt gymkhana. The children enjoyed the compact grounds which surrounded the house as they played tennis or walked family pets along the terraces, across the lawns and through the rose garden. From photographs Daisy the greyhound, Biddy and her puppy, as well as Bengy, seem to have been the firm favourites. Adults enjoyed evening strolls admiring the borders of spring and then summer flowers. Parties and balls were a feature of life at Penn Court. Guests expected to be well fed and they were not disappointed as the 1913 summer ball menu demonstrates.

Summer ball programme and menu, 1913

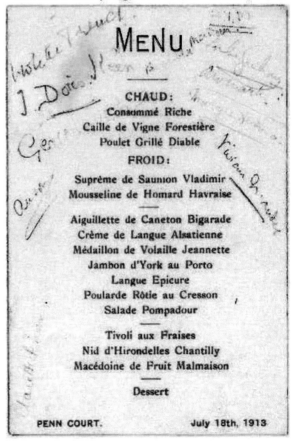

The social scene was completed by a string of family weddings. Miss Josephine Fox was married to Lieutenant GV Hickman RN; Miss Phyllis Lucy Hickman, daughter of the late Mr AW Hickman of Goldthorn Hill (died 1902) wedded Major James Deane CMG, of Fareham and late of the Black Watch Regiment. The ceremony took place at St Mary Abbots, Kensington.

Victor acquired the house known as Woodthorne at Tettenhall in about 1906. It was the former home of Sir Charles Marston, the founder of Sunbeam cycles, motorcycles and cars. Whilst a move was effected Penn Court was still retained, although an inventory of its interior (below) suggests it was no longer lived in by the family.

Furniture and household effects	£2193-12-0
Pictures	£211
Ornamental items	£170-14-0
Silver and Electro-plate	£210-8-0
Wearing apparel	£780
Linen	£100
China and Glass	£82
Books	£123
Cigars	£25
Total	**£3995-14-0**

The world was about to change when the Hickmans took the Villa San Giogio at Taormina in Sicily for the summer of 1914. The old order would never be the same again after the events that were about to unfold at Sarajevo. The resulting World War placed high demands on iron and steel producers and the Hickmans rose to the challenge. Doubtless the company made profits, but the Hickmans were very patriotic. With the mobilisation of troops in 1914 Victor immediately made the empty Penn Court available, and it became a temporary barracks for the 6th South Staffords. Two hundred soldiers were billeted in the house, outhouses, garages and grounds, where once the property had catered for no more than 20 residents and servants. Musketry practice was undertaken on the Sedgley rifle range on what is now part of Goldthorn Park. The Hickmans alongside most British families lost loved ones and were left to cope with the grief. Second Lieutenant Phillip Gregory Hickman, Victor's youngest son, died of his wounds on 31st October 1917 whilst serving in the trenches. A service at St Michael's and All Angels, Tettenhall marked his passing. A year earlier the wider Hickman family had mourned the death of Brigadier General Hugh Gregory Fitton CB DSO from wounds received in action in France. Born in 1863 he had joined the Royal Berkshire Regiment, afterwards serving with the Royal Warwicks and the Royal West Kents. He had taken part in the Egyptian and Sudanese campaigns including the battles of Atbara and Khartoum. In the South African War he was a staff officer. He rose to be an aide-de-camp to King Edward VII between 1907 and 1910 and held a similar position under George V. 1910 had seen his marriage to May, a daughter of Sir Alfred Hickman.

The Hickman family's links with the military were strong. Sir Alfred had had six sons. His heir, Alfred William, became managing director of the family firm, but died in 1902. The third son, Edward, had a commercial career with the company and first lived at Muchall Hall, before moving to Danescourt. But the second son, Thomas Edgecomb Hickman CB DSO, built a distinguished career in the army, rising to become a brigadier general. He served at the Nile, in Sudan and in South Africa. He gained the Distinguished Service Order in 1889 and became CB (Companion of the Order of the Bath) in 1909. In retirement he was an honorary colonel of the 6th South Staffords territorial force. He lived at Wergs Hall.

It is doubtful if Penn Court ever fully recovered from hosting troops. For a time after the war the house was let to Major Arthur J Holloway OBE. He had served in South Africa and was twice mentioned in despatches in France. In civilian life Arthur was a works contractor and a director of Wolverhampton Wanderers Football Club. By the early 1930s he had moved to the Poplars on the Penn Road.

The Wolverhampton Corporation Acts of 1926 and 1932 took Upper Penn into the borough, which resulted in a great period of house building in the former parish. Upper Penn became a favoured dormitory suburb. The Penn Court Estate, developed between 1933-6, became Osborne Road, housing well-to-do professional men and their families. Penn Court has slipped from our memory.

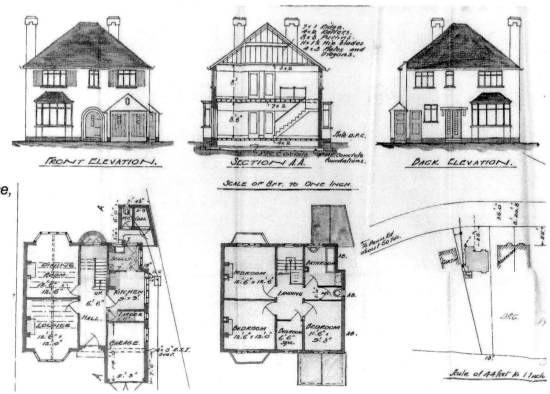

Architect's plans of Shutt Bros house, Osborne Rd

Tawny owl

Barn owl

78

For over 40 years I explored the byways and green lanes of south Staffordshire. I came to look forward to seeing one family of birds above all others, that of the owl. It has a special place in my heart for it enriches our lives with its presence. If we remain observant at least three members of the owl family can be seen and heard locally.

They are creatures that are perfectly adapted to exploit their environment. A number of an owl's physical characteristics make it a constant danger to its prey- its big eyes give it excellent sight; its large head, in relation to its body, and with ears on the side of its face, allow it to pick up and process a range of sound unavailable to us; its aerodynamically designed wings and cleverly arranged wing feathers enable almost silent flight.

The barn owl is perhaps the best known member of the family, although it is not the most numerous. Its ghostly white appearance makes it a bird of mystery and myth. This is easily understood walking from Blazebank across Hope Meadow to Orton at dusk, when its silent swooping flight suggests a ghostly apparition is at large in the valley. However, its aerial presence is more worrying for the field mouse, shrew, mole, rat, rabbit or evening swallow, as the barn owl will suddenly pounce upon one spot using the full force of its body to stun its victim, before completing the kill with its talons. In harder times the owl will feed on earthworms and beetles.

It is a bird of open agricultural land and rough pasture, the sides of Cann Hill and Foxhills and the open farmland to the west providing a perfect habitat for both owl and small British mammals. Just as its colour, white, provides it with an alternative name, so does the title, 'barn', associate it with agriculture. Unfortunately the barn owl has suffered from a loss of nesting site, as farm buildings have been knocked down or turned into 'des-res' for the escaping town dweller. There are many examples of this process across the landscape – at Bearnett, Pear Tree, Langley Hall, Manor, Orton Hall, Orton Grange, Whitecross, Penn Moor, Mount, Muchall, Coalway, Oxbarn and Newhouse farms. The removal of hedgerows to create larger arable fields and the extensive use of insecticide, have altered the balance within the food chain, which has let the barn owl go hungry. The action of nineteenth century gamekeepers was always a threat to the bird and the bad winters of 1947, 1962/3 and 1982 further reduced breeding populations. Little wonder that it is now a protected species. The good news is that its numbers are showing some sign of improvement.

From boyhood I learnt that the barn owl nested in a hollow tree, where it laid between two and eight white, almost spherical eggs. No nest material was used, but there were discarded food pellets in the hollow and sometimes the eggs would rest on these. Whilst the hen bird incubated the eggs the male hunted silently across Orton. Even when the snow was down it could be seen hunting, its keen sense of hearing allowing it to pinpoint an unsuspecting bank vole beneath the snow. Rain, however, reduced the bird's ability to hear and locate its prey and its young family would go hungry. For the owlets rain could well spell disaster for the weaker birds as shortage of food results in them being eaten by their stronger siblings. Nature can be cruel, but ensures that the strong have a better chance of survival. Barn owls often lay a second clutch, but the success of this brood depends on the weather and the lateness of the season.

The barn owl's spine chilling 'screech' provides the third name for this species and adds to an image of a ghostly presence. Barn owls will also communicate by hissing. Finding the owl's daytime perch was more difficult for a noisy eight year old, who tried to tread carefully through Blazebank before reaching the higher trees which were then at the head of the valley. On occasion I was rewarded with a view of the owl standing on a branch, its orange buff upper parts camouflaging it against the trunk. Only its pure oval white face gave it away, but it was pointless thinking it was asleep as when I got nearer it would turn its head through 270 degrees, without turning its body, to track my movement, before flying off.

Our most common owl is the tawny, wood or brown owl, so called because of its rufous, buff and brown colour and because it is a bird of our woodland copses, coppices, plantations and mature gardens. At about 15 inches long it is bigger than the barn owl and is a nocturnal creature seldom seen before dusk. These days I miss my walk up Springhill Holloway listening to it calling its mate with a 'hoot, hoot' through the autumnal equinox and well into winter. I often caught a glimpse of it on a telegraph pole or gate post as I reached the top of the ridge. I miss too its noisy owlets in May/June constantly calling the parent birds for food with a 'kiwick, kiwick' sound. In myth and children's tales its call is portrayed as a friendly 'tuwit-tuwhoo'. I miss it also visiting the gardens of Showell Lane where I would watch it alight on a beech or fir tree. But best of all was seeing it glide effortlessly through the glades of Ladywell Woods as if on auto-pilot. The tawny owl has a specific territory which it covers nightly. It appears to be able to build up a mind map of every tree, bush and obstruction through which it must negotiate. Its shorter wings give it this manoeuvrability.

Like its cousin it nests in a hollow tree and sometimes it will take over a squirrel's dray. Two to 4 faintly creamy almost round white eggs are laid in April/May. I quickly learnt that climbing the tree to get a look at them was not sensible, as the bird is fiercely protective and will attack. The owl's diet is similar to the barn owl, but it will take slightly larger birds such as starlings as well as squirrels.

In daylight hours the tawny owl perches on a branch tight up against the tree trunk. Motionless in a bolt upright position its colour provides perfect camouflage. The only time it is seen flying in daylight is when the weather is bad and it has gone hungry. A tell-tale sign of its presence in these circumstances is it being mobbed by dozens of small birds.

Our third owl is not a native of the British Isles being a nineteenth century import from Europe. Called the little owl because of its height at 8.5 inches, it is well established on agricultural land, where there are plenty of hedgerow trees. It favours parkland habitats, orchards and pollarded willows. I last saw the plump, squat-headed bird with no tail on a fence post in Wrottesley Park, as I walked our dog through deep snow. The little owl has greyish brown upper parts spotted and mottled and barred with white. Its bill is yellow. It is diurnal, hunting at dawn and dusk for field mice, shrews, insects, beetles and small birds. Its call is a 'cu, cu, cu' and its flight is erratic. Again this species nests in a hollow tree laying 2 to 5 dull white, but almost elliptical, eggs.

Where I live now I only see – or, more usually, hear – the tawny owl, but its presence is not so obvious. There is good news for West Midlands residents however, as the World Owl Trust is developing its new World Owl Centre in the grounds of Himley Hall, which it is hoped will open in 2017.

Little owl

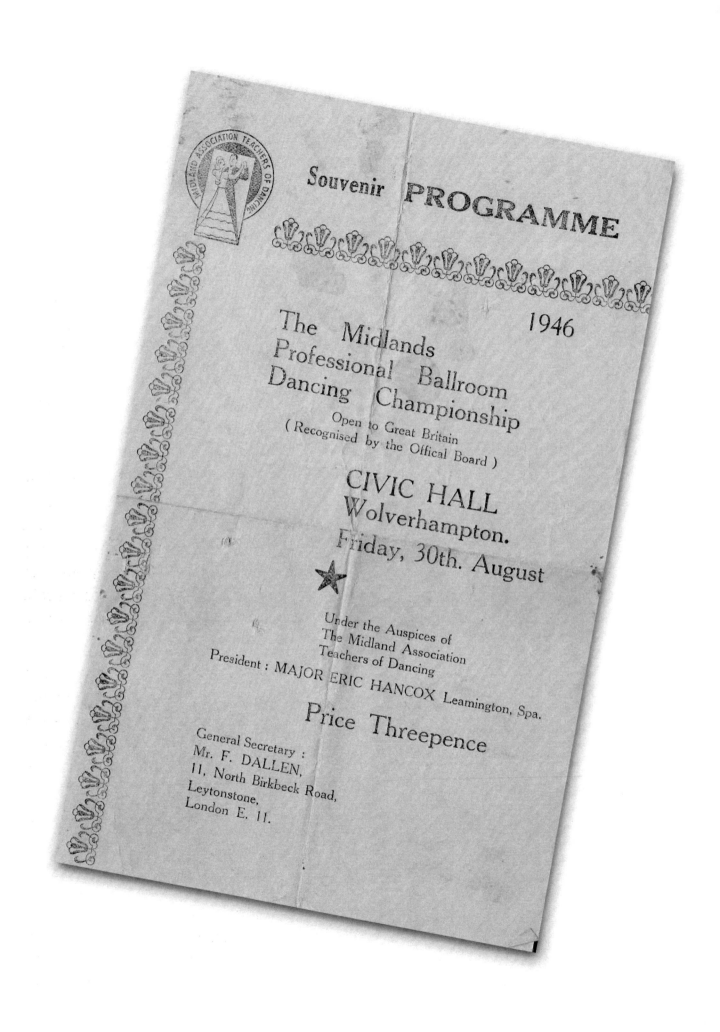

Souvenir **PROGRAMME**

1946

The Midlands
Professional Ballroom
Dancing Championship
Open to Great Britain
(Recognised by the Offical Board)

CIVIC HALL
Wolverhampton.
Friday, 30th. August

Under the Auspices of
The Midland Association
Teachers of Dancing

President : MAJOR ERIC HANCOX Leamington, Spa.

Price Threepence

General Secretary :
Mr. F. DALLEN,
11, North Birkbeck Road,
Leytonstone,
London E. 11.

Chapter 11
Angela Scott in the late 1940s:
diaries of post-war Wolverhampton

Miss Angela Scott was a Wolverhampton schoolgirl in the 1930s and 1940s, who kept diaries from the mid Thirties until at least the 1960s. They were found in the attic of number 133, Merridale Road during a house clearance and subsequently sold on eBay. No diary is complete and some have very few entries; nevertheless, they make fascinating reading. Through them, the reader may follow Angela's life, including a first-hand experience of Wolverhampton in the Second World War years – which I covered in one chapter of my previous book: Penn: Explored, Explained & Remembered.

We left Angela in 1945 having survived wartime Wolverhampton with all its perils and challenges. We saw how aware she was, as a schoolgirl, of the global war and how she took full advantage of the rich arts scene in the town, whilst at the same time gaining her school certificate and becoming a student.

Four of her diaries for the subsequent period have survived, those for 1946, 1947, 1948 and 1950. None of them have a complete set of entries – 1947 & 1950 have few – and there is a tailing off in the second half of each year. However, they do record her observations, opinions and values at a time of great social change and at a time when the British population was trying to work its way through the serious difficulties left by six years of world war. The diaries are particularly useful as they relate to Wolverhampton, then a major manufacturing town heavily bound up with helping rebuild the British economy. These years, for Angela, are years of further personal growth as she tests out her views and works out her future path.

Her week was busy and she had the foresight to cram in a wide range of courses at a very diverse range of centres. This demonstrated her determination and youthful endeavour. She took French and Russian at The Tec and for a time also studied German. These evening courses were usually held in cold and sometimes very cold rooms. Whilst group attendance was poor her attendance was exemplary and she was entered for RSA examinations. She had a low view of the Dutch until three Dutch boys enrolled on the Russian course.

She travelled to the Kings Heath area of Birmingham several times a week to study literary texts, learn her lines and act out the scenes. She was widely read. Her teacher was affectionately known as Hastie, but to some extent Angela was in awe of her. Angela's diaries often record, "Hastie in a bad mood" or "Hastie difficult". The journeys to Kings Heath were by no means easy. They were undertaken by either bus or train to Birmingham. The vehicles/carriages were always overcrowded and often ran very late. For the most part she used the GWR line to Snow Hill and commented that on one occasion it took only 20 minutes, whereas it often took more than double that. A walk and a further bus ride were required at each end of her journey. She usually caught the 17.40 from Snow Hill and once in Wolverhampton went on to her Tec course.

Dance classes were also forced into her schedule and with homework she was fully occupied. Her parents were very supportive and required little of her in the home and perhaps she did not always appreciate this.

In 1946 she was about 18. Her artistic interests are reflected in her BBC diary for the year. At that stage the BBC was not 25 years old. The first broadcast had been on November 14th 1922 from the London Station of the British Broadcasting Company; in the days that followed stations were opened in Birmingham, Manchester, Newcastle, Cardiff and Glasgow. September 28th 1923 saw the first issue of the Radio Times, but it was not until 1st January 1927 that the BBC received its Royal Charter. It was even longer before Foreign Language Services began, first with Arabic on January 3rd 1938, quickly followed by Spanish, Portuguese, French, German and Italian.

Angela was still heavily into listening to what she now called 'radio', rather than the former term 'wireless'. With her added maturity she was far more critical of what she heard and often expressed her reasoned opinion of a play or piece of music. Added to this was still some youthful worship of some of the stars of screen. It is clear that she was moved by some performances and that she was able to express her admiration in seeing them. She enjoyed the radio play *Memorial Concert* by Trudy Bliss in which Jill Esmond and Rosalyn Boulter starred. She could comment that the music by Arthur Bliss "was haunting". In the cinema she found Lilli Palmer and Rex Harrison's performances in *The Rake's Progress* "frightfully polished". Whilst she enjoyed *Brief Encounter* she thought it was spoiled by the use of Rachmaninov's piano concerto as background music! Often she would go with her mother as they both enjoyed the arts. She could also appreciate the power of political oratory and commented on the 5th March on Winston Churchill's speech at Westminster College, Fulton, Missouri, in which he introduced the concept of the 'Iron Curtain'. She expressed her excitement on listening to the Victory Day Parade in London between 10am and 1pm on 8th June. The family, glued to their radio, celebrated with bacon and eggs for breakfast and lamb and mint sauce for lunch, topped off with bread and butter pudding.

Angela took a number of stage magazines and began to apply to theatres for a position in their repertory companies. She applied in Wales and to Keighley, Bedford, Halifax and Bury amongst others, but with no luck. She had her portrait taken at Mayfair Studios in Wolverhampton and at Havana's, so that she could include a photo with her applications. She was invited for an interview at The Arts Theatre Company in Leicester Square and caught a 6.40am train from the High Level. She was badly let down as when she arrived she was told that they were sorry, but they could not help her. Rather than kick up a fuss she went and had a coffee and then went to Slaters in Piccadilly for lunch. One can't help admiring her style and resolve, but wonder if she was too nice about it all. There were further disappointments with an audition at the BBC in Birmingham, but no subsequent offer. She was it seemed offered a position at Wednesbury Rep but a few weeks later she received a letter saying "it was off". However, Angela although only 18 did not give up. She joined the Tettenhall Towers Theatre Club and attended their classes and undertook a number of supporting and leading roles. In rehearsals she complained that the boys did not sufficiently learn their parts – does anything change? She took the opportunity to unofficially explore the labyrinthine passageways of The Towers. Angela also performed at the Tec in Big Hall.

Socially she enjoyed meeting her girlfriends in the Liberal Club. Like most young women she was interested in shopping and in her appearance. Beatties and Bradfords in Victoria Street, Joan's in Queens Square, Jeanettes, and Marks & Spencers in Market Street were favourite haunts. Angela could comment that "Beatties buttered buns are marvellous"; Beatties had become a town institution, a social gathering place and an emporium of the best post-war products. She constantly hunted for overcoats, dresses and shoes, complaining that they did not fit or the colour was wrong. Icilma shampoo, which she said squeaked beautifully, and Cussons Imperial Leather soap were favourites when she could get them. Sometimes Angela would shop with her mother and they certainly shopped until they dropped, trying to get around the shortages which still remained.

The Towers, Tettenhall (below)

The Chimney Piece, Tettenhall Towers (below)

Rationing was still very much in force and caused huge difficulties for the population. There was a full scale debate in the Commons on the issue. Ben Smith, the Food Minister resigned in 1946 and was replaced by John Strachey. Exports were a priority so that Britain could begin to pay off its debts. As a result the availability of goods on the domestic market was heavily restricted. The soap ration was cut, as was the bread and bacon ration. With a hard winter with much frost and snow, followed by a freezing thaw there was real hardship and this on top of the seven years of wartime deprivation. Hollingsworth sausage, when one could get it, seemed to be a staple diet of the Scott family and Angela applauded "the jolly old sausage".

Dennis, their butcher at Bradmore did his best, but Angela on fetching the meat ration reported, "it seems to shrink a little each week". Queuing for food, sometimes for an hour or so, was a normal

'Russell' lupins

part of daily life. But the humour of the Wulfrunians broke through the gloom. On one occasion when Angela had queued unsuccessfully for sausage and had waited an hour in the damp cold she reported that a woman in the queue made the response, "it's enough to pinch the buttons off your coat". When Angela was successful, as was the case when she managed to get some liver from Lyons, her spirits were given a real lift. Bananas were now available if you were lucky and Angela shared one with her mother. Her father Pop's chocolate cake, when one could get the ingredients, was definitely a must.

To add insult to injury there were other price increases and some cuts in services. Train fares were set to go up on 1st July 1946 and Angela mused that the Birmingham-Wolverhampton return journey was likely to cost her 3 shillings and a penny. The electricity supply was cut on the 12th March and Angela reported that "most of the motor industry is stalling".

However, life went on and Pop began to distemper the lounge. As in all good comedies he managed to kick over the paint bucket, with adverse consequences for the carpet! But there were enjoyable days. On the 10th June Pop drove his wife and Angela out onto the Shifnal Road to see the wonderful sight of Baker's fields of lupins, with their

High Green, Tettenhall

rows of reds, oranges, yellows, blues and purples. Afterwards they stopped to walk on Kingswood Common.

Angela did not realise the advantages that her middle class home had given her. She adversely commented on the house building going on in Albrighton saying, "The horrid housing estates are spoiling the countryside." She failed to understand the need for decent social housing to provide fit and proper homes for those in need.

There were other outings. Mother and Angela caught the bus to Tettenhall where they found a "darling little antique shop" just off the Upper Green. It was still there in 1952, when as an eight year old schoolboy I bought a First World War French bayonet and a Paraguayan mate cup made out of a gourd. My mother confiscated the bayonet.

Angela had a real treat when she bought some Rowntree's of York chocolates from a shop near New Street station. In August Angela was driven to Low Level Station by Pop for her holiday with Joy and Harold in Portsmouth. She took the Paddington train, changing at Reading. She stayed in their flat, sleeping on the couch. She enjoyed walking along the seafront and seeing naval vessels including an aircraft carrier. Most of all she took pleasure in being treated as an adult, as was the case when they bought her a gin and orange.

Back home, the town Art Gallery was always an enjoyable experience and in 1946 there were two exhibitions which she particularly mentioned. The first represented the influence of American architecture by the use of skyscrapers, whilst the second was a joint Picasso/Matisse reproduction exhibition.

Angela took an interest in football and commented on Derby's success over Charlton in the 1946 FA Cup Final. This was the first such event since before the war and is famous as Bert Turner scored for both teams. Drawing at full time, Derby won 4-1 in extra time. Her other entry records a tragic event and one that has reoccurred at football grounds in our time. Bolton were playing Stoke in an FA Cup quarter-final at Burnden Park. The turnstiles were closed, but still supporters entered the ground. It is suggested that there were 85,000 present. With the crush 33 people died and over 400 were injured. The enquiry recommended that turnstiles be fitted with equipment which could record a permitted number of supporters and that major grounds be subject to police scrutiny over capacity.

One diary entry is of scientific significance. She recorded that on March 25th she attended the Towers Theatre Club and afterwards whilst returning across The Rock, she witnessed the Aurora Borealis, or Northern Lights. This is rarely seen this far south, although in February of 2014 it was recorded in Essex, Norfolk, Gloucestershire, North and South Wales, Northern Ireland and even in the Channel Islands. The spectacular displays are caused when the solar wind (electrically charged particles ejected from the Sun) enters the earth's atmosphere. It takes two or three days for it to reach earth and when it does it causes the gas atoms in the sky to glow. We witness continuous wavy bands of magenta, red, green and yellow light chasing themselves across the night sky.

There is little political comment in the 1946 diary. Angela does mention de Gaulle resigning in January and Stalin responding to Churchill's Fulton, Missouri speech by calling for an inquiry into alleged

British troop misconduct in Indonesia. She also mentions the start of a Russian withdrawal from Persia (Iran).

Coming from her comfortable middle class home it was probably inevitable that she had little regard for the Labour Government. She called Atlee "that silly little man", and criticised Bevan for his housing policies. Her family attended a public meeting at the Civic Hall called by John Baird MP, representing the then Wolverhampton East constituency. She was pleased to say that they had great fun shouting him down, although it must be said that at least she took part in the political debate, unlike so many today.

The dominant theme in her 1947 diary was the extreme weather which Wolverhampton, with the rest of Britain, experienced. Snow, thaw, freezing thaw, blizzards and high winds were recurring themes throughout the first four months of the year. The unpleasant and sometimes life-threatening consequences were corporation transport suspended, power blackouts, fuel shortages, intense cold in peoples' homes and a population that looked "more like polar bears trudging through the snow than Wulfrunians". Angela reported that at times the Austin works at Longbridge was closed due to cuts in electricity supply, RAF Cosford sent its personnel home on extended leave as base fuel supplies ran out, Britain had suffered from 40 days of continuous frost by 25th February 1947, England was cut in two by blizzards on 5th March, and a hurricane hit on 16th March.

Angela put the seriousness of the situation into context when she said that "after the worst of the blizzards, snowdrifts in some areas were as high as the telegraph poles and householders had to cope with burst pipes, with rivers running down the streets from Central Wolverhampton". As if this wasn't enough the thaw brought with it yellow fogs to add to the discomfort. With the evening the pavements refroze. Angela sipped her Horlicks by candlelight.

1947 was a year in which Angela made progress with her shorthand and typing classes. She also travelled to Birmingham to take stagecraft lessons with Mrs Morrison. But, she found time to shop for shoes in Craddocks at Snow Hill, Wolverhampton and to take coffee at Aldridges, in both Lichfield and Victoria Streets, and Reynolds in Queen Square. The Co-op, although Britain's largest food retailer, with many additional consumer lines, did not appeal.

Angela continued to develop her artistic interests by supporting theatre and cinema, borrowing books from the Central Library and travelling to Dudley Library to see the Rembrandt exhibition. She continued to follow the Wolves and noted that they played Staffordshire rivals, Stoke.

There are brief references in the months of June and August to the glorious summer of that year, but unfortunately no detail. However she went to the seaside in June.

1948 was a special year for the country, for Wolverhampton and for Angela. It saw the silver wedding anniversary of George VI and Elizabeth Bowes-Lyon and the birth of their grandson, Prince Charles, the nationalisation of the railways, the staging of the Olympics, and celebrations of Wolverhampton's Centenary of Incorporation as a borough. This allowed Wulfrunians to elect 36 Councillors, twelve Aldermen and a Mayor. For Angela it was also the year she started her first job.

Angela welcomed the nationalisation of the railways, probably because her experience of travel from Wolverhampton to Birmingham was so bad. However, she did not realise that what the railways needed was massive investment in both networks and rolling stock. Public ownership would not instantly improve these. She commented, "A great day for the railway companies – they now belong to us". Neither did Angela make the link with Labour policy for she heavily criticised the nationalisation of coal. She delighted in Labour's by-election defeat in Calmachie and in the rough ride Food Minister John Strachey had in his own constituency of Dundee. She rejected the move to a National Health Service, but recognised Aneurin Bevan's quality when she reported, "he did not spare anyone's feelings." Her sympathies were with the Conservative party. She joined the Young Conservatives and was at a constituency meeting when John Enoch Powell was adopted as the Conservative candidate to fight the Wolverhampton South West seat at the next General Election. She was pleased at one of Churchill's broadcasts and wrote in her diary that "he gave the Socialists a whipping".

Like for the rest of the population the shortage of food was an even more important element in her life, as the following diary entries demonstrate:

- On January 4th 1948, "lunch was a queer happening – such peculiar meats – a relic of the blitz – it looked and tasted rotten. No pudding – no flour."
- On the 16th January, "mother dashed off to Hollingsworths to get some sausage for lunch."
- On 31st January, "tried my luck in the sausage queue, but not a link available."
- On 2nd February, "Potatoes scarce."

Whilst the most telling comment of all simply stated on the 3rd February, "I am hungry".

Later in the year, with coupon changes things were a little better and certainly there had been an improvement over the war years.

Bus fares went up in 1948. Angela complained in January that she had to catch a replacement "horrid Don Everall coach" instead of the Corporation bus. In the late 1940s Britain could not meet the demand for public transport. There were simply not the vehicles available as the export market was all-important with Britain in a dire financial state. It would take until the early 1950s before sufficient new vehicles could be made available from town suppliers like Guys (motor and trolley buses) and Sunbeam (trolley buses). In the meantime Wolverhampton was lucky in that it had two considerable private operators in Everalls and Worthington Motor Tours, who between them leased twenty to thirty vehicles to the town, even if they had seen better days.

In Wolverhampton, as in the rest of Britain special stamps were issued to commemorate the Silver Wedding of the King and Queen. It was also the centenary of Wolverhampton's incorporation as a borough. On 17th March the Centennial Industrial Exhibition opened in the Civic Hall. Between May 22nd and June 5th, Wolvehampton's Centenary Pageant was performed at the same venue. It was written by L. du Garde Peach, produced by T. Heath Joyce and the music was composed by Percy M. Young. With 18 scenes, it told the colourful story of the town from the gift of land by Lady Wulfruna in the 10th century, through the centuries, with the finale proclaiming the great industries of the borough. It had a cast of hundreds.

Centenary pageant programme, 1948

In May there was a glorious Centenary Flower Display in front of the Victorian Town Hall. In June the family went to the Municipal Airport at Pendeford to see the Centennial Air Pageant. The day was hot, but fortunately a light wind blew.

1948 also marked the celebration of the Civic Hall's first 10 years. It had provided the venue for many of the most important cultural, artistic and political events in the town. On 19th December Arnold Richardson gave a recital, which included Bach's 'Jesu Joy of Man's Desiring'. The popular *Down Your Way* radio programme came to Wolverhampton to add to the Borough's celebrations.

But 1948 was also the year of the British Industries Fair at nearby Birmingham, which the King and Queen attended. Angela's loyalty to her home town allowed her to enter in her diary, "all the flags out there, but it does not look such a treat as Wolverhampton, especially at the GWR station – it's just dandy"! The following day she read the write-up in the Express and Star, which featured Mr FP Webster's (of Spinning Ltd) presentation to the Queen. She had bought a pressure cooker from the company stall.

Toward the end of the year the Duke of Edinburgh visited. Angela first saw him in Queen Square. Outside the Civic Hall she listened with the waiting crowds to the proceedings, which were relayed by loudspeaker. In the afternoon she saw the Duke being driven past the Grammar School, with its lines of cadets and schoolboys. She took a photo, no doubt on one of those ex-RAF 620 films she had purchased cheaply earlier in the year and which were the first films available to her since before the war.

Internationally 1948 meant the Olympics in London. Angela, like the rest of the nation was captivated by it as it represented a coming together to jointly

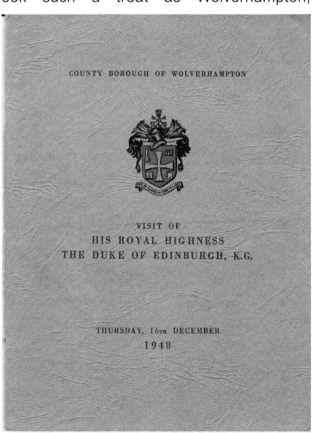

Programme for visit of HRH the Duke of Edinburgh, 1948

celebrate human achievement after years of strife. It did much to keep morale high. She could appreciate the achievement of Fanny Blankers-Koen of the Netherlands, whom she thought came second in the 80m hurdles, but in fact the photo-finish showed had won gold; plus Catherine Gibson winning her heat in the 400m freestyle, and Reg Harris's achievement in winning two silver medals in the cycling.

For Angela Thursday nights became theatre or concert nights. On 18th March she visited Birmingham Rep to see *The Shop at the Corner*, whilst the week before she visited the Grand to see the ballet. In April she was at the Civic Hall when Norman del Mar, Sir Thomas Beecham's understudy, had the baton. Her musical repertoire was extended by listening to the radio. She listened to Beethoven's Symphony No 1, overtures by Wagner and the Symphonic Espagnola by Lalo. 1948 was the year she discovered Shelley. Cinema still held an attraction and in May she watched *Road to Rio*. She also saw the film *My Brother Jonathan* adapted from the book by Halesowenian, Francis Brett Young. Her comment was, "saw a grand film; all about the Midlands; Wednesbury was in it. Michael Denison was very good."

1948 was the year Angela found employment. She had been attending Barclays College in Queen Square and was up to 160 words a minute over 5.5 minutes with her shorthand. Her father had fixed up an interview at Spinning LtC. She was appointed and in early March entered the typing pool. Her comment at the end of her first day was, "too tired to do anything when I got home". Reality had begun to dawn. She complained she no longer had time to read the papers and that she did not like the work. However, over the following weeks she boosted the number of invoices typed per day from 106 to 130, to 160. She felt her shorthand was not being fully utilised and eventually persuaded Mr Goodwin to use her ability. She was transferred to a tiny office as a stenographer, but she missed the music which was played in the typing pool. But there were good things too. She was proud that she had paid her first shilling into the pools syndicate. She was trained in May on the use of the dictaphone. One of her managers left for a job which he said had twice the salary. Fridays were of course her favourite day as it was pay-day and this allowed her to spend a considerable amount of time shopping. The weeks began to slip by and it was soon Advent. On Christmas Eve she met up with her friend Betty. Betty told her she too was fed up with her secretary's job and Angela thought that it was about time that Betty made up her mind as to her future. This must also have caused Angela to think seriously about her own position.

Angela joined the Caledonian Society and enjoyed the socials and the Scottish dancing. She was also a regular member of the Young Conservatives, who met in Central Hall in School Street. She was still interested in football and was pleased when a friend sent her a programme of a Wolves friendly match in Holland. She also felt for "little Colchester" of the Southern League, who were beaten by mighty Blackpool in the fifth round of the FA Cup.

Unfortunately the 1949 diary is missing as she must surely have eulogised over Wolverhampton Wanderers lifting the FA Cup, by beating Leicester City by 3 goals to 1. The 1950 diary has few entries but it is clear that she had rethought her future and with a grant from the Education Authority returned to studying music and drama. It is of no surprise to see that the diary was 'The International

Film Diary', with lots of photos of the current stars of the day – Myrna Loy, Paula Valenska, Anna Neagle, Jean Simmons, Ann Todd, Margaret Leighton, Margaret Lockwood, Jean Kent, Betty Grable, Lana Turner, John Mills, Jean-Pierre Aumont, Burgess Meredith, Rex Harrison, Robert Donat, Bing Crosby, Alan Ladd, Tyrone Power, Gregory Peck, Ronald Howard, Danny Kay, Eric Portman and Michael Wilding.

Angela took a course in Birmingham which included the history of dance, dramatic characterisation, mime and improvisation. Her horizons were stretched further as she became familiar with such authors and playwrights as Chekhov, Voltaire, Joad, Tennyson and Maupassant. The services of the Central Library in Wolverhampton provided her with many texts and she became even more well-read and knowledgeable. Radio continued to play an active part in her life and her diary has comments such as "loved the story, it fascinates me". Her musical repertoire also increased with her regular visits to the Civic Hall and listening to classical pieces on the radio. Cinema too, an old favourite, was much enjoyed as she commented on the huge queues at the Savoy to see *The Third Man*. Of Jean Cocteau's film *La Belle et La Bete* she said, "it was pure poetry, I cannot remember seeing a film of such beauty before". The Odeon in Skinner Street was the venue for *The Spider and the Fly* and *The Life of Riley*. On a lighter note Frankie Howerd made her laugh.

Whilst continuing to keep her shorthand going at Queens College she balanced it by joining the Fencing Club at the Tec. It appears she was not a 'natural' at it, but benefitted from RAF instructors.

In January 1950 she voted for the first time in a General Election for the new Wolverhampton South West constituency. It is not difficult to guess how she cast her vote. This was the year Enoch Powell became her MP, taking the seat with a slim majority of 691. He was to hold this seat until 1974.

Angela continued to watch the Wolves and was pleased when they beat Sheffield United by 4 goals to 3 in the cup. She was less pleased in her entry when they lost 1-0 to Blackpool in the next round.

Angela knew now that her future life lay in some aspect of the arts. Over the next few years she would follow the path which would eventually lead her into teaching music and drama in one of the town's secondary modern schools.

Orton Hall farmhouse in the 1920s (above), and the same southern aspect in modern times (below)

Chapter 12
Restoration at Orton Hall

The liberty of Orton has long been a farming community with its collection of 18th century Georgian farmhouses and associated barns and cottages. In 1872 the hamlet supported a population of 197 souls who worked the land. At harvest times this number was swelled by itinerant workers. Gypsies regularly camped here for a few weeks at a time taking on jobs around the farms, but also taking time to make pegs and baskets for sale in nearby towns from hedgerow and bankside hazel and willow. As the centuries have passed the old barns and granaries are no longer fit for modern agricultural needs and there is always a potential conflict between replacing with modern plant, or, protecting the architectural landscape.

In 2009 Orton Hall Georgian farmhouse and buildings, which lie on the west side of Orton Lane where it meets Flash Lane were put up for sale as a development opportunity. The farm buildings included a threshing barn and stable with a loft over, a two-storey barn with a granary above approached by an external flight of steps, a dairy and cowhouse built onto the halls frontage, a five-bay open cattle shelter, and, at the rear of the house and garden, a stone and brick building dating from at least the 17th century.

Orton Hall Farm

Granary

Dairy & cowhouse

Threshing barn

Farmhouse

Orton Hall lies at the crossing point between Trysull and Wolverhampton and between Wombourne and Pattingham and is most likely the site of the Lord of the Manor's medieval hall. The site dominates the entrance to the Showell valley. The Georgian south face of the farmhouse has the inscription:

Sr
R:W
1754

This reflects the Wrottesley family ownership of the lordship, which they were not to relinquish until the sale of their southern estates in 1929. Sir Richard Wrottesley of Wrottesley (1721-69) was at one time Dean of Worcester Cathedral. 1754 would have marked the rebuilding or upgrading of an earlier hall. The Wrottesley family often incorporated date stones into their buildings. This period was at the start of the industrial revolution when progressive landlords and their tenant farmers introduced new hardier crop strains and the rotation of crops and introduced livestock breeding programmes to increase food production. Towards the end of the 18 century and up to the middle of the 19th Mary Tongue, probably connected to the Wrottesleys through a previous generation's marriage owned Orton Hall and extensive lands beyond.

The proposed development site plan suggested making three accommodation units out of the extensive 'L' shaped farmhouse; a unit out of the front dairy/cowhouse; a unit out of the threshing barn; a unit out of the granary building; and a unit out of the 5-bay open cattle shelter. The seventeenth-century stone and brick building would be turned into a garage by increasing the size of the aperture on its north western front. This would alter the visual impact of the most important building in architectural terms in the Orton Hall complex. It is not to be underestimated what can be achieved through goodwill and co-operation. A telephone conversation with the planning authority conservation officer and his intervention with the developers, who had already been granted planning permission, led to an historic building appraisal by a firm of experts, Stephen Price Associates Ltd of Worcester.

Their report commented upon the construction of this building, its main features, its possible former use and made suggestions as to the way forward. The north-west face of the building was of sandstone and largely complete, with a filled in three-light window above an enlarged door aperture. The window had a wooden lintel below which two slender octagonal mullions created three spaces. This feature goes back to at least the 17th century and is repeated across Orton Lane in the west face of White Cottage. The experts have dated a similar feature at Wribbenhall to 1665, although the form was about from the sixteenth century.

The building's west wall is of orange brick similar in nature to that of the 1754 farmhouse. Before restoration it displayed a bricked-up doorway at ground level, a large doorway at first floor level and a wooden framed opening under a segmented arch at second floor level. However, its most attractive feature was its ramped-up gable end with stone cappings.

West elevation of building

Appearance	Family member	Where
S^R RW̄ 1747	Sir Richard Wrottesley Born 1721 Succeeded as 7th Baronet 1742 Died 1796	Netherton House, 302 Bridgnorth Rd, Wightwick
S^R R W 1749		Seisdon Mill House
S^R: R:W 1754.		Orton Hall farmhouse, south front
S^r J +W 1827	John, Lord Wrottesley Born 1771 Succeeded as 9th Baronet, 1792 1st Baron Wrottesley. Died 1841	Heath Mill, Wombourne (demolished)
I L W 1842	John, Lord Wrottesley Born 1798 Succeeded as 10th Baronet, 2nd Baron 1841 Died 1867	Farm buildings, Trescott Grange, Lower Penn

Access drive and eastern face of farmhouse

Western aspect of farmhouse

Orton Hall farm buildings before restoration from Flash Lane

Looking east along Flash Lane, rear of cow shelter

98

Threshing barn with granary alongside

End view of granary

Five-bay cow shelter

*South face, Orton Hall farmhouse
with granary & threshing barn*

Northwest front of seventeenth-century stone and brick building before, during and after restoration (left)

Its three-light window before restoration (above)

Similar windows are seen at White Cottage (below)

The southeast elevation was largely obscured by an ancient yew and the disintegrating lean-to roof of a former orangery. Again the ramped-up gable end and stone cappings was in view, whilst the southeast wall itself was cement rendered to give the illusion of stone blocks. Butting the northern side of the east elevation is the brick perimeter wall (not shown) which links the stone building to the farmhouse.

The report found the building:

• To have been much altered over the centuries and probably to have originally extended further west

• To have had at some time three storeys

• To have had several uses over time, which included a storage barn for cheese and grain as suggested by evidence of remnants of a plaster floor; as an accommodation block for workers as suggested by a later hearth and chimney.

• To have undergone major changes, probably as a result of Lord Wrottesley's improvements in 1754, which included the addition of an orangery (?).

One wonders if indeed the building is the remnant of the medieval hall at Orton?

South elevation showing yard wall and doorway

In the event all the work of planners, architects, historic building appraisers, developers and council have ensured the retention of this seventeenth (sixteenth?) century building by allowing it to be converted into a modern dwelling, but retaining its stone features, its three-light window and its ramped-up roof with stone cappings. The derelict orangery has been converted into a timber garden room. A sensible solution has incorporated the former 19th-century WC building to the left of the structure, and to the right of the building the brickwork of an extension tastefully blends with the original stonework. The ancient yew has been retained.

Orton Hall and its buildings are in good shape for another generation or two and their pleasing visual impact will continue to grace our countryside. Orton hamlet still has farming connections, but the agricultural labourers of the past have been replaced by those who work in the conurbation.

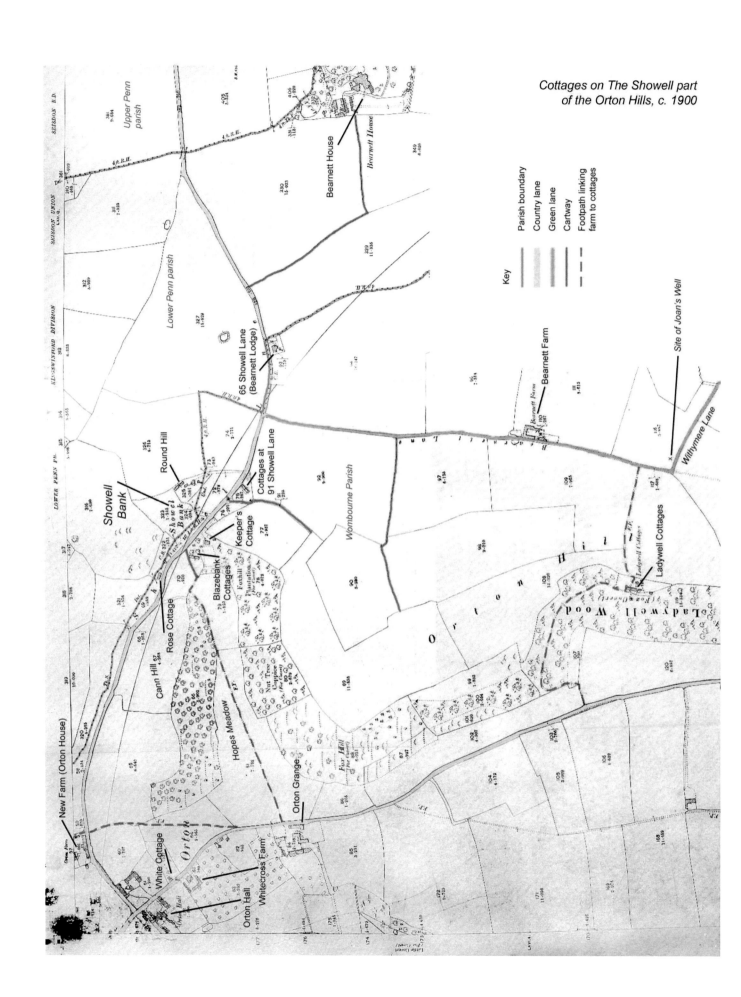

Cottages on The Showell part of the Orton Hills, c. 1900

Key

- Parish boundary
- Country lane
- Green lane
- Cartway
- Footpath linking farm to cottages

Bearnett House

65 Showell Lane (Bearnett Lodge)

Showell Bank

Round Hill

Cottages at 91 Showell Lane

Keeper's Cottage

Blazebank Cottages

Rose Cottage

Cann Hill

Hopes Meadow

New Farm (Orton House)

White Cottage

Whitecross Farm

Orton Hall

Orton Grange

Bearnett Farm

Ladywell Cottages

Site of Joan's Well

Withymere Lane

Upper Penn parish

Lower Penn parish

Wombourne Parish

The above names were all in common usage by the farming community until recently. They refer to a patch of countryside which traverses the Orton Hills from Lloyd Hill on the A449 trunk road to Orton hamlet's crossroads of Flash Lane/Orton Lane/Showell Lane. 'The Showell' was a term which referred to the many cottages which once existed along Showell Lane and on the adjacent hills; it was in effect a district on the Penn/Wombourne parish boundary. Some say that the name comes from the Anglo-Saxon, 'Seofan Wyllan', meaning seven wells, others that it stems from the word 'Shoal' – in the 1826 Assessment for the Relief of the Poor for Orton Liberty and on the 1808 Enclosure Award map, field numbers 279 and 280, which lie either side of the Lane and just above the entrance to Keeper's Coppice, have the names 'Upper Shoal Bank' and 'Shoal Bank Piece' or 'Siden Hill' (Sunken Hill, i.e. a Holloway). A *shoal* is a slope, and what a slope Showell Bank presents. Another field up on the plateau, number 270, is called 'Old Field' or 'Shoal' or 'Showell'. It lies to the west of Bearnett Lane and above Ladywell Wood and Hopes Meadow, the ground dropping away to Orton. This may well be the true meaning of Showell.

Others still claim that the word Showell originates from 'Sewells' meaning scarecrows, which were erected in the fences of enclosures in the medieval forest, thereby frightening the deer and keeping them in the forest. It is certainly true that the Orton Hills were part of the Wood of Putley, itself a part of Kinver Forest in this period. We have plenty of evidence of local men brought before the forest courts for taking the King's deer in the Wood of Putley. A few would say that Showell means 'show well', as in the case of the Ladywell, but this is less likely. Whatever the origin of these words one thing is certain – that the Orton Hills are known for their springs, as water seeps out where the overlying coarser Lower Keuper Sandstones meet the smoother-grained bright red Upper Mottled Sandstone.

At the sale of the Bearnett Estate in 1924 the land fronting the eastern part of Showell Lane was sold to property speculators for onward sale for housing. In the next fifteen years houses now numbered up to 51 were built on the southern side, with the exception of Westons; and up to number 30 on the northern side, with a few additions such as Borth further up the lane. After the Second World War further building took place and infill continued to Bearnett Lodge (No.65 Pen-y-Bryn) on the south aspect of the lane and to the crest of the ridge on the north side.

Showell Lane was a well tramped country lane from home to field and from farm to cottage. A well-established rural community lived on and around these hills, many cottages housing large families. The rural economy supported labouring families, through farm and estate work, with tied housing and large cottage gardens. Today these cottages have been rebuilt, enlarged and gentrified. This western part of the lane still retains a country air, only broken by the rush-hour commuters travelling into and from the conurbation.

65 Showell Lane, with its original chimneys (top), with them removed c.1981, and as it is today (bottom)

The tythe was originally a tenth payment on the produce of the land. The Tythe Commutation Act of 1836 introduced a monetary payment and detailed maps of each parish were drawn up, showing the land owner, occupier, land use, and the small and great tythes payable. As the parish boundaries ran across the western portion of Showell Lane it is necessary to examine the 1840s tythe maps for both Wombourne and Lower Penn parishes. They give much detail as to who was living where. Additionally, the 1841 census detail is of use.

Each of the cottages will be dealt with in turn and Bearnett Farm and Ladywell Cottages will be included because they were part of the wider Showell scene. No.65 Showell Lane was not built until after 1871, when it was called Bearnett Cottage or Lodge. It was built in the same pseudo-Elizabethan style as Bearnett House on Lloyd Hill, which was built by 1864 on the site of Putley Villa, which dates from 1854. The Lodge housed the estate gardener and his family. Water was supplied from a cast iron pump situated in the yard. Each weekday he would walk along a cartway which ran from the dip in Showell Lane across the fields to Bearnett House.

In 1901 Bearnett Cottage was occupied by William Hughes, aged 65, and his wife, Elizabeth. Their son Evan aged 26 lived with them as did William's nephew Thomas Outer (39) and niece Mary Still (22). It was quite common for a household to include members of the extended family and this could also increase the householder's income. Evan was a mechanic at a tubeworks and Thomas a boot and shoe factor. As can be seen the bond with the land was already being challenged.

In the period up to the sale of the Bearnett Estate in 1924, Ernest Rogers and his wife, Eliza, lived here. As head gardener he produced some wonderful displays of orchids and grew bananas and exotic ferns in the hothouses at Bearnett. From at least the 1930s until the early 1980s the Cummings family from Neath lived there. They called their house 'Pen-y-Bryn', meaning head of the hill. They extended the house, keeping the same style. Subsequently they returned to South Wales.

A few hundred yards further on is the junction with Bearnett Lane, a farm access and public right of way. The farm buildings, which lay somewhat along the lane, were probably built in the Napoleonic era, when Britain was trying to increase its food production, as continental markets were denied to it. A large barn, farm worker's cottage and farmyard sheds made up the complex. A garden pump connected to a deep well supplied household needs – the perfectly cylindrical bore through the underlying sandstone was the work of a craftsman. The only other water supply was from a very large cistern which collected rainwater from the cottage roof. Two small ponds with brackish water lay either side of the lane. Further away, where Bearnett Lane meets Withymere Lane lies Joan's Well, a natural spring on the dip slope of the escarpment. It is likely that there had been a cottage here, but not for the last 2 centuries. Apart from water supply Bearnett Farm suffered from another problem. When heavy snow fell the lane became blocked for days or weeks on end, making it extremely difficult for those who lived and worked here.

Bearnett House orchid house, 1920s

In 1826 Bearnett Farm was owned by Miss Tongue of Orton Hall Farm. She still owned it in 1841, when it is listed in the Orton tythe accounts as Bearnett Homestead, occupied by Joseph B Green, who farmed several of the nearby fields on his own account. By the time of the census in that same year Bearnett Farm was being worked by a farm labourer, David Stokes. With him was his wife, twenty years his junior, and their two-year-old son, also named David. It was quite usual for established older men to marry younger women. Also at Bearnett was Martha Wanklin, aged 17, classed as a servant but probably a relative, and her brother John aged 10.

Bearnett Farm up until the 1950s was always farmed from one of the Orton Farms – Orton Hall, Whitecross, or Orton Grange. In 1901 William Payne, a farm labourer, and his wife Eliza, lived at Bearnett. They had both been born in Shropshire and were in their forties. They like many others were part of the eastward drift of population towards the towns of the Black Country and the farms on their green borderland. Mr Owen, who worked for Mr Pothan who farmed

Bearnett banana house, 1920s

both Whitecross and Bearnett farms, lived at Bearnett Farm in the period of the First World War. He is seen in the 1920s photo of threshing the corn at Whitecross and is the operator of the stationary steam engine.

From before the Second World War until the late 1970s, the Degg/Minnett family were employed to work Bearnett. Harold Minnett and his wife were the last to reside there and Mrs Minnett would uncomplainingly carry the weekly 'shop' all the way from the bus terminus at Springhill Corner. In recent decades the farm has become part of the Wodehouse Estate and is farmed from Smallbrook Farm in Wombourne.

Bearnett Farm buildings, 1970 (above),
and sketched before demolition (right)

Orton Grange Farm (bottom right)

Ladywell Cottages, 1924 (below)

Threshing machine at Whitecross Farm, Orton, c 1920

On top of rick
1 Mr Jones (Mr Pothan's brother-in-law)
2 Horace Owen (lived in cottage in farmyard opposite Orton Hall

In front of rick
3 Laura Law (lived in 2 cottages which are now 'Orton Manor'
4 Ruth Piper
5 Mrs Piper
6 Edith Sadler (aged 14, maidservant, Whitecross Farm)
7 Agnes Rogers
8 Mrs Eliza Rogers (wife of head gardener, Bearnett House)

On top of threshing box
9 Teddy (son of Mr Piper)
10 Mr Piper, with sheaves of corn (lived at cottage between The Grange and Whitecross)

Below
11 Tom Piper

In front of engine
12 Mr Pothan (former Whitecross Farm; he also farmed Bearnett Farm)
13 Mr Owen (engine driver, lived at cottage at Bearnett Farm)
14 Mr Tom Law (lived at White Cottage next to nursery)

To the south west of Bearnett Farm and across the fields by a footpath lie the foundations of Ladywell Cottages, which housed two labourers' families until just before the Second World War. The cottages, built of sandstone blocks cut from a small quarry at the top of the Orton Hills lay in the wood on the scarp face of the hill. In 1841 they were part of the Reverend Dalton's Lloyd Estate and were occupied by the families of Edward Tucker and William Williams. By 1871 there were still two labourers' families, but this time the occupants were George Williams (possibly a relative of William), his wife Harriet and their daughter Sarah, all born in Wombourne; and Ann Walker, the Head of her household and an agricultural labourer in her own right, together with her son Richard, who was then aged 18. The Walkers had both been born at Donnington in Shropshire. Their water supply was from the Ladywell, a natural spring issuing forth at the junction where two sandstones of different textures meet. Above the rock face and clinging to it is an ancient yew. At the age of eight I would climb it and sit on the platform at the top of the tree. Here a wonderful vista was set out to the west. One could watch the tractor in the fields at Orton, the express goods train disturbing the summer air as it made for Crewe along this rural branch line, or listen to the woodpecker's *'rat tat tat'*, as it searched for grubs in a nearby tree. The Reverend William Dalton, of Lloyd House, had built a summer house nearby, so that he too could benefit from the vista and the glorious sunsets, but unlike the yew tree platform it has long since rotted away. In the dark days of World War Two the Home Guard and Sergeant Bloxham would keep vigil at this highpoint, watching for enemy paratroopers. They did not see any, but they did see and report waves of German bombers on their way to and from Liverpool. As the field path enters the wood to the left are the remains of the cottages' gardens and the damson orchard. Many a pie has been baked from this fruit by those lucky enough to know where to look.

Before returning to Showell Lane, the high point of the Orton Hills is passed, marked by a trig point at 535 feet above sea level. At the junction with Showell Lane is an expensive property which dates from the 1970s and which was originally built as two labourers' cottages to replace Bearnett Farm cottage.

New cottages, Bearnett Farm

Showell Lane becomes Showell Bank as the steep scarp face drops away. On the left at what is now number 91 were a further two labourers' cottages. In 1841 Hannah Jordan, a widow aged 75 and her 40 year old son, Joseph, a farm labourer, occupied one of the cottages. Mary Williams, another widow, but aged only 59, and her three children, Joseph aged 20, Sarah, aged 19 and Prudence aged 12, tenanted the other cottage. By 1871 Richard Palmer, his wife and five children lived in the one cottage and Martin Finn and his wife in the other. Martin was 60 and had made the journey in his younger days from County Mayo, Ireland.

On the right of Showell Bank the driveway to Round Hill breaks off. This was where in the nineteenth century Charles Whitehead, the wheelwright, lived with his wife Mary and four children. He had been born in Penn, but his wife in Newport, Salop, demonstrating the influx of people from Shropshire and the Welsh borders. Charles' skills were much in demand on the neighbouring farms, as they knew he kept their wheels turning.

Halfway down Showell Bank and on the north side is the Showell Spout (now behind the bridge of the private drive to Orchard Hill, which was not built until 1937). The Spout was the water supply for the cottages which lay on the hill and the occupants would have to carry it pail by pail. The stream from the Spout runs down through the garden of Rose Cottage at the base of the hill before vanishing into the dry Showell Valley, and then reappearing in the ponds of New Farm (Orton House). The 1826 Assessment for the Relief of the Poor surprisingly suggests that Plot 282, which includes Rose Cottage, consisted of 3 houses, land and gardens. They it says were occupied by Joseph Jordan, Joseph Williams and Richard Nicholls. Two of the buildings, if indeed there were two, are lost in time and to view. In 1841 Widow New (Mary, aged 60) resided at Rose Cottage and tended her

A beauty spot: Keeper's Cottage from Hopes Meadow (top), the White Cottage in the Orton Hills, and 'Cottage at Orton' water-colour by WJ Bradney, 1908, showing Keeper's Cottage and Blazebank (bottom)

garden there. Her 17-year-old son, James, again an agricultural labourer also lived there.

A little below the spout and to the left is the access drive to Keeper's Coppice (Cottage), where the estate gamekeeper resided. The house is not shown on the 1841 tythe or listed in the 1871 census. It was built by George Ward for his gamekeeper. In 1901 Thomas Garner, his wife Mary and their children, Joseph Robert, aged 10, and Lily aged 3, lived there. Joseph had been born in Wombourne and Lily in Pattingham, which suggests a recent move.

A watercolour of the property painted from Cann Hill in 1908 is shown. Blazebank was then a row of labourers' cottages, and a part of these is also represented in the painting. The sandstone for Blazebank Cottages was cut from the top of Cann Hill, and a depression now marks the spot. Between Blazebank and Cann Hill was a cartway giving access to Hopes, the meadow which runs down to Orton Lane and Orton Grange farm. It is a dry valley. In 1826 William Jordan and Benjamin Williams were labourers living at Blazebank. They still occupied the cottages in 1841 working for Mary Tongue at Orton Hall Farm, the major landowner in Orton hamlet. By 1871 William Bentley, a shepherd, his wife Jane and their 3 children, Mary Ann, Ellen Maria and Thomas William were living there, whilst the other part of Blazebank housed Joseph and Mary Williams, who were both in their forties.

The Orton community depended on the landowner who rented out his farm on an annual tenancy, but in practice the tenants remained for many years. They hired in labour at one of the farming Quarter Days of the year, Lady Day in March being a favourite. Whilst many labourers stayed put, the pull of better wages in the expanding town of Wolverhampton and sometimes a better pay offer on other farms meant that there was a turnover of labouring families. The census returns for the late 19th century show that workers were being drawn in from Shropshire and Worcestershire and that there was also an Irish presence, presumably from those who came to do seasonal work and then stayed. Orton at times had a gypsy encampment and farmers welcomed their presence for the work they did. The women used the withies from the hedgerows for basket-making and the hazel for making clothes pegs. Labourers worked long hours on the farm, and apart from horse-power all labour was manual. The wives often worked in the farmhouse kitchen and laundry, stone-picking in the fields in January, and helped in getting in the harvests of the various crops. Their wages were much less than those of the men, but the demands were equally taxing.

Whilst the farmer travelled to Wolverhampton for the weekly market, labouring families had to find their pleasures nearer at home. For the children there were chores, but they had the countryside to explore and other children to play with. A Sunday school was run by Mrs Jenks in her kitchen at Orton Grange Farm. St Benedict's in Wombourne and, from 1888, St Anne's in Lower Penn village offered the usual support and special services on high days and holy days. Great emphasis was placed on the village show, and there was keen competition from labourers to gain prizes for the produce of their cottage garden. National events were celebrated and marked in both Wombourne and Penn villages. For school, St Benedict's and the Penn Winn Endowed School (St Bart's) at Springhill (until 1871) provided a basic education. Children would be missing at harvest time.

However, times were changing. There are still families in our midst whose forebears tilled these lands. Their testimony, together with the 1901 census, provides a picture of what life was like. Living at Rose Cottage was widow Mary Laws, then aged 67, her daughter Clara Ann and her son Edward. He was a groom and domestic servant, probably at one of the farms and if not at Bearnett House. Anne Brown of Brown's Nurseries recounts that her grandparents, Thomas and Alice (his second wife) Pace and family, lived at Rose Cottage in the early years of the 20th century. Grandfather Pace worked as a labourer at Orton Grange Farm. Their cottage was still known as Pace's right up until the 1950s, when the Walkers moved in. Anne's father, William (known as Bill), was the youngest of the Pace children. As was all too common in those days, his mother died in childbirth and he was lovingly brought up by his stepmother Alice. Bill was to become a farm labourer like his father, working first for the Yorks at New Farm and then for Mr Pothan when he was at Orton Grange. Bill married and lived in one of the two cottages which became Orton Manor. His wife sold teas to holidaymakers, for Orton was a popular spot in the summer months for daytrippers until after the Second World War.

Pace's Cottage was known for its watercress beds, fed by the Showell stream, as well as for its mock-orange tree with its glorious Whitsuntide display. Anne Brown reminds us that the garden apples tasted better than any ever bought from a greengrocer. It is said that the privy was in the garden astride of the Wombourne – Lower Penn parish boundary. What Anne

Thomas Pace, Rose Cottage

does not know is that in June of 1877 a large party from the Naturalist and Archaeological Club of the Wolverhampton Free Library visited the Ladywell and the Orton Hills. They stopped for tea at Rose Cottage to find "a long table spread out in the garden with plentiful fare, and plenty of watercress from the brook close by". After the picnic the Reverend FS Johnstone read his paper on the Triassic sandstone formations of South Staffordshire. The party then walked back to Bradmore and Wolverhampton.

Thomas Pace & second wife Alice on unmade Showell Lane outside Rose Cottage c.1910

The Adderley family probably lived at Blazebank Cottages and it looks as if they took up all the accommodation. Samuel, aged 48, had frequently moved his employment as he tried to better himself and provide improved conditions for his large family. His children's places of birth illustrate some of his moves – Claverley, Bobbington, Worfield, Penn. In 1901 Samuel was a shepherd on the Orton Hills employed by Mr Jenks of Orton Grange Farm. He had moved from Langley Hall Farm where the farmer had been Mr Beddard. Samuel and his wife Elizabeth (Lizzie) had eight children, and seven were living at

Blazebank. Their ages ranged from 21 years down to 3 years. The eldest, William, who didn't live at Blazebank, was already established as a farm labourer. Like most British families, their sons – three of them – were to fight in the Great War. One, Richard Thomas, always called Tom, served in the Australian Army and more importantly survived. Before the War he had been regarded as the 'black sheep' of the family. Tragically, in 1904 Lizzie died in childbirth aged 45. The child also died. Samuel, whose life ended in 1918, had built up an estate worth over £1000 net. He had taken a 21-acre smallholding at The Drivefields off Langley Road from Staffordshire County Council and also become the manager of Seisdon Rural District Council's sewage works at Merry Hill. Many of his family were to work in the nearby town as the old order gave way to the twentieth century. Some of his descendants still live in Penn.

The Showell may have become gentrified, but the rural past remains part of the landscape, at least for a little while longer.

Penn Secondary School as part of Colton Hills Comprehensive School

The population of the Staffordshire parish of Over or Upper Penn had continued to grow through the first few decades of the twentieth century. The 1902 Education Act made fundamental changes to the way in which education was delivered in England in that school boards were swept away and their functions transferred to county councils, county boroughs and urban districts. These bodies could use the rates to support both former board schools and voluntary schools. As the state increasingly took greater control of education it had to provide greater opportunities for the young. The 1902 Act allowed for secondary provision. It brought about a national system of education and over time provided a ladder of opportunity for the young. The Fisher Act of 1918 consolidated this national approach by fixing compulsory school attendance between the ages of 5 and 14. Village all-age schools would take up this challenge but many with limited buildings and expertise would be hard pressed.

It was in this climate that Penn's Senior school was conceived and built by the County education authority to provide both a general and practical education for three year groups of 11 to 14 year olds. It was given the county school number of 408 and its standard number (maximum roll) set at 480 students. It opened on 1st September 1932 with 4 female and 5 male staff, plus Mr Allen as a part-time member. Mr LJ Richards, the headteacher, was part of the complement. At a staff meeting that day the aims of the school were set out and the work discussed. Children arrived on the 5th of the month, transferring from a number of Penn Elementary schools. They were allocated by age to one of six classes. The County allowed the school to include overage children. The Reverend Hartill, Vicar of Penn, called with the parental consent forms of children transferring from St Bartholomew's Church of England school, who would attend the parish church for Tuesday morning service between the hours of 9 and 9.30am. Mr J Lakin, a County Councillor, together with a deputation from Wombourne called to see the headteacher with a view to admitting children from that parish. These subsequently joined, being Staffordshire children, as did one from Seisdon.

Like all new schools there were teething problems. Much of the physical training equipment was still awaited. Some of the dinner boys were making a nuisance of themselves. The ditch in the garden had been used as a drain for the nearby piggeries, creating a health risk.

That first Christmas term ended with a party which ran between 3pm and 9.50pm on 22nd December. A tradition had been established. In subsequent years there would be an event, for both the younger age group and one for the older pupils, which included a fancy dress parade.

With the new term in January came a new set of challenges. Tiles had blown off the roof above the emergency room, there were frequent breakdowns in the heating equipment which resulted in poor attendance figures, and these were exacerbated by severe snowstorms. The Reverend Hartill complained that attendance at Tuesday morning prayer in St Bartholomew's church had dropped off. Alongside all this there were the usual visitors to the school: medical staff (two children found to have 'nits', three were untidy and two had long hair), juvenile employment officers advising the leavers, and the Director of Education for Staffordshire, Mr FA Hughes. Members of his department also frequently visited as did His Majesty's Inspectors of Schools.

On 1st April 1933 the parish of Upper Penn moved into Wolverhampton County Borough, along with the school which fell under the control of the Wolverhampton Education Committee. It was given a new number – 52 – and was renamed Wolverhampton Manor Road Council School. On 22nd May the Director of Education, Mr Warren, spent an afternoon in the school. This term saw the second edition of the school magazine, the mowing of the playing fields (the motor mower broke down and a horse mower was brought in to save the day), pupils taking part in the Wolverhampton Schools' Sports Meeting, a netball tournament, 33 pupils attending the residential school camp at Kingswood, and the appointment of prefects – three girls and three boys. At the school's own sports the boys' Under-13 80 yard dash was run in 10.6 seconds and the girls' race was won in 11 seconds. The Over-13 80 yard hurdles was won for the boys in 11.6 seconds and for the girls in 12.6 seconds. The girls raced in an Over-13 80 yards and the winning time was 11 seconds, whilst their 100 yard race saw a winning time of 12.4 seconds The boys' half-mile was won in 2 minutes 33 seconds. Other events included the high jump at Under- and Over-12 and a boys' Under-13 80 yard hurdles. Mr Richards declared himself as highly pleased with the standards achieved.

The motor mower had been out of action for much of the term. After a visit at the end of term by the then Mayor Sir Charles Mander and Councillor Smithies, the school received a Ransome 14-inch mower for the caretaker to operate. Its limited size must have reduced its effectiveness. It succeeded in mowing the boys' football field, but failed to cut the long grass on the girls' field. The term closed with an annual Bible and prize distribution, the Winn Endowment actively playing its part. (Charles Winn, Vicar of Penn from 1646-69 left monies in his will to buy the poor children of Penn bibles). In the 1930s the summer vacation lasted only for the month of August.

At the start of Manor Road Council School's second year the school roll stood at 306 children, which showed it was at 64% of capacity. However 119 new children had been admitted and the roll was growing. Attendance was given a high profile and at the start of the year it was 95.1% with a figure of 94% obtained for the Christmas term. The year began with flooding in the girls' cloakroom and repeated boiler breakdowns, which were to repeatedly bedevil the school over the coming years. Indeed on the 12th and 13th of October 1933 there was no heat available. Pupils and staff stoically got on with the business in hand. Once pupils were 14 years of age they could leave school, so each year had 3 leaving dates – Christmas, Easter and summer. The school roll fell by 22 for the spring term 1934.

As the school settled down a number of features became evident. Wolverhampton was a well run authority whose officers regularly visited the school, watching lessons, checking the log book and registers, discussing with the headteacher relevant matters and checking equipment. In addition the authority appointed school visitors from the local community who took a keen interest in the life of their school. The links with the Winn Endowment remained strong both through the headteacher's commitment as a board member, the support of the education authority and the Reverend Hartill's presence just up the hill. In July of 1934 66 leavers received Bibles and 8 prizes awarded.

A feature of the curriculum was the use of the locality and places of interest for lessons. 40 girls were taken on a nature study ramble through Baggeridge Woods, Penn scholars represented their school at the Wolverhampton Music festivals, swimming was undertaken at the Central Baths. In 1934 138 children visited the Staffordshire Agricultural Show, whilst 82 children journeyed to London and visited St Paul's, Westminster Abbey and the Tower – all in one day! In another year 89 pupils, 9 staff members and 5 parents visited Bristol, Wells, and Wookey and Cheddar. 68 children and 18 adults made it up Mount Snowdon. There were many trips over the years to see Shakespeare at various theatres, including Stratford and the Grand in Wolverhampton. Pupils enthusiastically attended lectures at the Technical College and at the Baths assembly rooms on such topics as aeroplanes and electric lighting. Mount Road Council School obtained its wireless receiving licence. Evening picture shows in school were ever-popular, as were the promotional films of the London, Midland & Scottish Railway (LMS) – visiting north Wales, visiting London, and The Royal Scot Train. 1935 was the year of the Royal Silver Jubilee of King George V, and Penn students played their part in the pageant (as 30 'peasants' and 25 'rats') put on at Molyneux Grounds. A special bus was provided to take them and return them to Penn once the show had finished at 10.30pm. Those children living at a distance from Penn were escorted home by a member of staff.

Staff too were encouraged and supported on a wide range of training courses, both short course and longer term ones, and the school quickly developed a reputation for developing the talents of its workforce. During its first dozen years several staff were promoted to headships of town schools, including Miss Padfield to Graiseley, Mr Shelley to St Bartholomews and Miss Fryer to the senior assistant post at Elston Hall. Mr CCJ Brown representing the NUT was a member of the Teachers' Consultative Committee, which regularly met the Director. He left at the end of August 1943 to take up the leadership of Willenhall Road Senior Boys' school. Miss Humber had moved in 1942 to take up the headship at Stonefield Junior and Infants at Bilston. Mr Brown (affectionately referred to as "Buster" in the privacy of the staffroom) along with Miss Padfield were to figure in post war Wolverhampton as the very well respected heads of Bushbury and Prestwood Road Secondary Modern schools. The headteacher attended a Board of Education fortnight's course in Cambridge. At a more fundamental level Manor Road school was used by Dudley Training College as a suitable place to train its teachers. Whilst students occasionally came from a range of other providers the Dudley link was particularly strong and Dudley relied on Penn when it needed to give a student who had experienced difficulty elsewhere a second chance.

March 1934 saw the last submission for places by out-of-borough children, thereafter Wombourne and Seisdon pupils being directed to Penzer Street, Kingswinford. Mr Richards complained that within the borough he was not allowed to take female pupils from Coalway Road and Trysull Road, which gave the school an unbalanced profile in the younger age groups. There were 40 girls but 88 boys in the bottom four classes by age group. In September 1935 the school roll had increased to 348 but the number of girls was only 140.

The usual range of misdemeanours were reported as a few students were caught stealing, fighting with Graiseley boys, throwing stones at gas lamps or petty-pilfering at the town's baths. There were a few more serious cases where the police and magistrates were involved and which led to a pupil being placed in care at the Cottage Homes. On a sadder note a couple of boys witnessed a fatal accident on the Penn Road, which in those days was quite narrow and with an increasing volume of traffic.

The headteacher in planning for the third year of the school discussed plans with the staff. There was a general opinion that the work pupils were asked to do by the different subject teachers could be more homogeneous and provide a more coherent experience. It was felt that the craft work that children were asked to do needed to both stimulate the children's interest and have a useful purpose for them as individuals. Social activities were to be broadened and the older children were to be given more responsibility, which would help them take on the role of useful citizens. Already pupils were looking after chickens and selling eggs. They also processed honey from the bees they kept, although on one occasion the teacher had been badly stung. During the war these activities would be extended to running a pig club, whose members would benefit from the meat produced as did the Ministry of Food. Rabbits were also kept.

The headteacher was certainly at the top of his form. In January of 1936 he set up with the Director's support a parent-teacher association and quickly enrolled 120 parents. The Reverend Hartill was the PTA's first chairman. A series of exceptionally well attended educational evenings, social functions, garden parties, sale of work, and school events followed. The PTA, in what were harsh economic times, repeatedly raised funds for school equipment. There was a Dramatic Section of the PTA and in 1938 they presented The Dear Departed and A Thread of Scarlet, at which 200 people were present. A dietetic course was arranged for parents.

On 22 January 1936 the school assembled in the hall to listen to the Proclamation of Accession of King Edward VIII. The assembly was concluded by singing the National Anthem. On 28th January the school was closed for the funeral of King George V. The school was again closed for the Coronation of George VI in 1937.

This report was given at a time when the British public were suffering from severe hardship. To put it in context, even in an area like Penn, in September 1936 the school medical officer informed the headteacher that there were 47 children undernourished, i.e. 1 in 7.

It was at this time that the school adopted a British tramp steamer through the Ship Adoption Society. The vessel was named the Harpagon. It was built at Lithgows Ltd on the Clyde for J & C Harrison Ltd in 1935. On May 13th 1942 Mr Britton, secretary of the society, spoke to the children and they were thrilled at his stories of their ship. He passed on the personal greetings of Captain RWE Laycock and his crew. However, what Mr Britton and the school did not know was that the SS Harpagon, while unaccompanied on a voyage from Baltimore to Barry some three weeks earlier, had been sunk by a U-boat 100 or so miles off Bermuda. 41 out of 49 in the ship's complement, including the captain, were lost. On the 15th of July 1943, Captain Laycock's sister and Mr Britton visited the school to unveil a photograph of her brother. All these events must have brought home to the children the terrible price paid in war.

Penn's Senior school was doing well and was regarded very favourably by the Education Office in North Street. At various times heads of other schools such as St Joseph's and St Peter's Girls visited, as did representatives from outside the borough. Exchange teachers from South Africa and Australia taught at Manor Road for a few weeks.

By 1938 at national level the 'additional year' for all – a fourth year of senior schooling – was being talked about. This however, would be interrupted by the war. There was some improvement in facilities at Penn: extra sewing machines, a projector and a piano. The school was now using BBC wireless broadcasts as stimulus material for such things as Armistice Day. Special lessons followed which brought home to the children the significance of the day.

Students regularly sat for places at the Art School and Manor Road built a reputation for a high standard of work. A student from Oxford visited and the headteacher reported that both he and the pupils had a great morning. The head was keen to provide role models and to give encouragement. However, he also had to deal with the mundane: a broken nose of one of two boys fighting, the first graffiti to appear in the newly reconditioned toilets, an angry parent whose daughter had been sent home because she was "verminous", boys misbehaving in church.

Manor Road Council School was inspected in March of 1939 by His Majesty's Inspectors (HMI). The report noted that its location was on the outskirts of the town near an area of great housing activity. It also noted that the children came from both rural and urban homes and therefore the school needed to offer a wide range of activity to meet their needs. The headteacher was praised for "rising to the opportunity very successfully and for his commonsense, driving force and ability to develop his staff. There was continuous growth and improvement in the school." It stated that great thought had been given to organisation and to the machinery for seeing that it fulfilled its purpose. Out-of-school activities, the PTA and measures for children's self-government all came in for praise. The school was it said already working toward providing for the raising of the school leaving age through its four-year course. HMI noted the difficulties caused by the imbalance between the number of boys and girls. French had been recently introduced for some pupils with success. The report then went on to examine subject by subject. The teaching of science and art received high praise. Comments to do with English and Maths reflected the gender issues seen in our own day. Less able children were treated with kindness it said, but there needed to be a greater expectation placed upon students. The Director was delighted with the report and the school's success.

By September of 1939 Britain was at war with Germany and Manor Road moved towards its wartime arrangements. Four air raid shelters were completed by the end of October and eight by early November. Air raid drills were held and gas masks checked. Some were too small and others were perished. Replacements were eventually provided through the police. The Director, Mr Warren, visited the school and spoke to the children about their work for War Charities. Knitted garments were sent to the Red Cross. Fourteen parcels of cigarettes and sweets were sent to Old Boys serving with HM Forces. £2-13-7 was sent to the Express and Star Fund.

As the school re-opened for the January term in 1940 staff shortages had begun to affect the smooth running of the school; they were to get worse as men were called up. The commercial work in the leavers' class was abandoned. Blackout was put up in the laboratory and coal supplies frequently ran out. The school would be without heat for a considerable number of short periods over the war years and the headteacher had to adapt the timetable accordingly. On January 12th 1940 there was no central heating and the office was contacted. The Wulfruna Coal Company then delivered 2 tons 12 cwt of coal but this ran out on 15th January. On 19th January accommodation was found in the dining room for one class from Woodfield Avenue until their air raid shelters were completed. With a severe winter these were extremely difficult times, when the motto was 'Keep open for as long as you can and run a normal timetable whenever you can'. Taking children on a walk on a very cold morning or afternoon session became part of the timetable as did setting work for children to do at home and bringing in a limited number of year groups at a time. Attendance suffered.

Mr Charles Mander visited the school to talk to the children about the National Savings campaign. Parents were invited to a wartime cookery demonstration taking place at the Technical College. Keeping rabbits was added to the food-producing activities of the school. The headteacher, keen to keep up morale and raise the spirits of the local community started an Old Scholars Association. About 80 turned up for the first social. Subsequently drama, puppetry, model aeroplane making and science clubs were run.

From August 1940 the school stayed open during August particularly for families where both parents were at work in the town's factories. Staff took holiday leave on a staggered basis. On Sunday August 25th there was an air raid which lasted from 10pm to 4am on Monday 26th. Only 96 children were present on the 26th. Children were advised to bring to school a rug/blanket and pillow in case they needed to sleep in the day, as their nights could be sleepless. Air raids continued on the night of the 26th.

Air raid sirens became a regular feature of the coming months and years. The week of October 4th saw 3 such warnings, and calmly filing into the shelters became part of their working week. The weeks of late 1940 and early 1941 were particularly bad for the number of air raid warnings. In December a party of children visited War Weapons Week exhibition in town. Pupils found a film show on the role of anti-air raid measures instructive, entertaining and inspiring.

Apart from this school was normal. Painters were in painting the top corridor and the medical officer's staff were carrying out their checks. However, painters' rubbish was left in the boiler house and the caretaker was not careful when raking over the hot ashes. As a result the rubbish ignited and smoke came through to the hall and science laboratory. At this time there was an air raid warning, but quick action in true Dad's Army style, with the help of a bucket chain of boys and a stirrup pump, doused the considerable flames.

In early October 1941, to coincide with Wolverhampton's Food Week, the school put on displays and events: Miss Barnett the Cookery mistress gave daily demonstrations at 2.30pm, garden produce was on show in the art room, the Thrift Club displayed handmade garments, Miss Red had a miniature model of a ship convoy and Mr Shelley presented – through world maps and coloured ribbons – the danger to British shipping. Between 3.20 and 4.30pm parents and visitors were entertained by the pupils. After the week's events a clothing parcel was sent to the school's adopted ship. At the end of October 1941 permission had been granted to farmers to employ school children in school hours for potato picking, but only it was learned later with Ministry of Agriculture permission. A year on, the children were shown colour films of fruit growing, tomato growing, pests and diseases and winter storage.

The headteacher made the emergency room available at night for fire watchers. In the spring of 1943 some of the school fencing was removed for the war effort. Mr Richards was requested by the education department for 50 messengers with cycles in case of an invasion. The messengers would work with the police and would be on duty on one day each week from 9am to 7.30pm. Warships Week was the 23rd March 1942 and Able Seaman LT Kendrick visited to talk to all the children. Later in the week 200 children visited the exhibition in the Civic Hall.

In April 1943 Mr Richards complained in his log at the large number of windows broken by stones thrown during the Easter break and the fact that horses had been running over the garden. The residents of Butts Road were singled out for taking short cuts across the school garden to the corner of Manor Road. May 1944 saw 'Salute the Soldier Week' celebrated and Captain Brandon Thomas came to talk to the children. The Bourneville mobile film unit visited to show a film called When We Build Again which raised in a positive way the new opportunities that hopefully lay around the corner. In June education officials interviewed those children who under circular 1654 were recommended for further education. July saw the admittance of 81 evacuee children, about half coming from Barnstead, Surrey.

The continual pressure on headteacher and staff did not lessen with the start of a new academic year in September 1944. Staffing remained an issue as it had done throughout the war. There were now 98 evacuee children; there were two streams only in the first and third years; there were 49 'B and C' children in form 8 and 55 in form 2; there were 53 'A and B' children in form 1. Grouping of boys for PT in the 3rd year gave a class of 51 and in the final year a class of 59! Added to this the weather was inclement and no heat was available. The Optimist Clubs of Canada and the USA kindly donated free chocolate to the evacuated children. What did local children think?

With the dawning of 1945 only 24 evacuees remained. January brought severe weather and by the end of the month ice was inches thick in the boys' toilets. Even hot brine could not melt the ice to flush the pans.

On 17th May the school was closed for the pm session so that pupils could attend a thanksgiving service at the Molyneux Grounds at 7pm. The first bus left Penn at 5.30pm and returned 3.5 hours later. Many children who had been on their feet for all that time fainted and one child had to be brought home by ambulance. By the autumn the school was able to operate a little better. 311 children travelled to the Odeon in Skinner Street to see Laurence Olivier's Henry V. The wartime attendance of concerts in the Wulfrun and Civic Halls was continued when a party travelled to listen to the Jacques string orchestra. In December 1945 the children entertained a party of Dutch children. This was part of the Wolverhampton-Tilburg link which came about from Wolverhampton's association with the Royal Dutch forces housed at Wrottesley Park during the war.

The headteacher Mr Richards had been interviewed in 1944 for a seconded post for duty at an 'emergency training college', which would train over a year mature men and women to fill gaps created by the teacher shortage. It seems likely that this was the post to which he went as on 6th May 1946 Mr Thomas Gifford Daffern commenced duty as the temporary headmaster.

Mr Richards had established Manor Road School as a successful senior school in the town. He had won the trust of the local community and had created a workmanlike and happy atmosphere for children. He and his staff had been highly praised in 1939 by His Majesty's Inspectorate. The war years had been particularly challenging and whilst times were still austere and the challenges great, it was a time for further rebuilding. The school was already fulfilling much of the Butler Education Act of 1944, which regularised compulsory education for all between the ages of 5 and 15 and which placed the secondary modern school as the route most children would take. The best practices of Penn senior school could still be seen in the way the best secondary modern schools operated in the town until they were swept away in the early 1970s by comprehensivisation.

The far western end of Lower Penn parish is in the shape of an arrowhead. The northern boundary is the Smestow Brook, which at times of heavy rain is a fast flowing sheet of water, whilst to the south lies Ebstree with Bates Farm, known today as The Hollybush, dominating the skyline. These two axes are joined by a parish boundary cutting across fields of wheat, barley, potatoes and oilseed rape. Near the arrow's head lies the busy farmyard of Furnace Grange together with its barns, sheds, farmhouse and cottage.

The Smestow Brook at Furnace Grange

The river terraces of the Smestow valley provided early man safe and productive settlement sites with easy access to water, but well above the flood plain. In dry summers secrets long hidden sometimes emerge as patterns appear in the fields. This is the case on Furnace Grange's lands, where hut circle outlines of possibly the late Bronze/early Iron Age can be distinguished. Flux from their cinder pits has been excavated. This is not the only evidence available. Aerial surveys have shown crop marks in a field close by Pool Hall. A flint scraper found in 1963 on the hills near to the Park Hall hotel on the Wolverhampton/Sedgley/South Staffs boundary was dated to between 6000 and 8000 BC. So we can see that some of the lands in and about Penn have had a human presence for at least 10,000 years.

Recent excavations have also uncovered a Roman marching camp, across the brook from Furnace Grange in a field alongside the Bridgnorth Road. This area was at the Roman frontier in the period AD 47 to AD 61. Marching camps were quickly thrown up to protect their forces as they moved from place to place. They would have been abandoned as the column moved off on its next operation, but they could also be re-used as needs required. Several marching camps have been identified along the various roads that emanated from the Greensforge Roman forts – three at Greensforge itself, two on the west side of the Smestow between Checkhill and Camp Cottages, and one at the top of Swindon Holloway.

The Roman road from Pennocrucium (Stretton/Gailey) to Greensforge passed down through Pendeford and whilst it remains lost between there and Hinksford the discovery of the Furnace

Grange marching camp suggests that the road may well have followed the Smestow valley down through Compton, Wightwick (local folklore has given part of the land between these last two settlements the name of 'Roman Cemetery') and Trescott, before crossing the Smestow. The road would then have travelled via Ebstree, Trysull, Swindon and Hinksford to Greensforge.

Further evidence of Roman occupation in this district was discovered when in 1700 a labourer found a Roman golden torc hidden beneath a boulder in a field in Pattingham. This was probably hidden in a time of trouble by a Romano-British colonist, but it could also conceivably lend support to a settlers' trackway across the Tettenhall plateau via Great Moor and the Blackbrook valley.

For its early history Grange Furnace must be seen in conjunction with Trescott Grange. The foreword to the first volume of the printed Penn Parish register tells us that "in 985 King Ethelred granted one manse at Trescote to Lady Wulfrun, who appears to have granted it in 994 to the church of Wolverhampton". After a spell out of church ownership, William Buffary, Lord of Lower Penn, granted the lands around Trescott to the monks of Combe Abbey in Warwickshire. They built their grange and lay brothers and/or their serfs farmed these lands, stocked their fishpond and tended to their dovecote. It was quite usual for a medieval noteworthy to give lands in perpetuity to the church, so that the monks would pray daily for his soul. Such gifts were seen as less welcome by the deceased's relatives, whose inheritance had been curtailed. They often challenged the gift in the courts. Such was the case with William's widow, Sibelle, who on 8th July 1200 petitioned that some of the Trescott lands belonged to her. Abbot William Fitz Widow, not wishing to be seen as disinheriting a widow, promised her 20 shillings and 8 pence yearly; but the lands remained the property of the church.

The monks also built a mill, which would not only grind their corn, but provide revenue from the serfs, cottagers and villeins. Many were the disputes concerning mills and their water rights. Ralph de Perton, who owned the next mill upstream, admitted that he had withheld an adequate supply of water from Trescott mill. Almost 100 years later, in 1272 Roger Buffary sued Philip, Abbot of Combe for a messuage and 6 virgates of land, and a mill at Trescott. The abbot defended his right and the case was adjourned. Quite where the mill was is open to conjecture, but it was possibly at the Furnace Grange site. Indeed over time three mills were to operate somewhere on these lands.

Six centuries later the 1843 tythe map of Penn still gives a clue to the establishment of early farming, for the field patterns display an irregularity of shape and a bigger acreage than those fields which lie eastwards beyond Pool Hall, which portray a planned and organised set of boundaries and shapes.

This western part of the parish remained agricultural and in church ownership until the dissolution of the monasteries, when the Crown usurped the property. It was later sold to William Wollaston in 1557 and a descendant, Hugh, died possessed of it in 1610. Dr Peter King in an article on Grange Furnace in The Blackcountryman (summer edition of 2008) has suggested that the blast furnace which was built on the banks of the Smestow might have been built by William Wollaston (died 1604) at the same time that he acquired a mill at Orton (probably Heath Forge at Wombourne) in 1584 from John Grey, Lord of the manor of Orton. However, firm references to Grange Furnace do not begin until 1636 when a case was brought against Richard Foley for unfair practices in buying up all the cordwood he could, and thereby depriving his competitors of the means to produce iron.

Within living memory and probably for a few centuries before, a shallow phlegm (fleam, leat or millrace) took water from the Smestow below Perton Mill, where a weir in the river provided a head of water. Water flowed a considerable distance along the 300-foot contour, crossing Ford Lane on the bend (here a further weir returned excess water to the brook), flowing beneath the brick cart bridge below Trescott Grange, and through 'Phlegm Meadow' to Furnace Grange yard. In summer with generally slower flows and warmer weather the ditch could smell badly and residents of Trescott would complain. Here the water fed the millwheels on an overshot system, before being returned to the Smestow.

Certainly by the early decades of the 17th century the charcoal-fuelled blast furnace was in production, using a waterwheel and a gearing system to compress alternatively two large bellows. These would have blown air into the furnace causing the burning charcoal to reach very high temperatures. A huge area stretching from Newport in the north to Bridgnorth in the west supplied Grange Furnace with the necessary charcoal. Iron ore was transported by pack animal from the Wednesbury/Bilston coalfield and limestone, for use as a flux, from the Dudley/Sedgley hills.

The furnace would have been square in construction, its hearth made from fire-resistant natural rock. This may well have come from the Triassic sandstones of Himley or from the top of the Orton Hills. The hearth was approximately two feet across, but as the furnace rose in height so the internal gap widened. At the opening a connecting ramp would have allowed labourers to tip in barrowloads of ore, charcoal and limestone to keep it topped up. The hearth would have been tapped every 12 hours or so and the molten iron run off into channels in the receiving sand beds, known as sows and pigs. The cooled iron was thereafter known as pig. The present farmer tells of a large ingot and several smaller ones being uncovered when the cottages adjacent to the mill were extended and turned into one residence. This gives us the likely furnace location.

The cottages are the oldest properties on the farm and this probably means that this was where the bellows were situated. Between the present mill building and the cottage is a bank of clinker, the stony residue of a furnace. Indeed the tythe survey fields, which lie between the mill and cottage on the one hand and the Smestow on the other, are named 'Cinderbank' and 'Cinderbank Meadow'.

The 17th-century iron industry on the banks of the Stour valley

Clinker at Cinder Bank

system of streams is inextricably linked to the Foley family. Their commercial prowess saw Richard (1558-1657), a former nailer, mechanise the slitting process. His third son, Thomas (1616-1677), continued to build their influence. Grange Furnace was purchased in 1639 by Thomas Foley and his brother-in-law, William Normansell, for £600 from Peter Hassard and Henry Wollaston of the Fishmongers' Guild and from Richard Wollaston, citizen and vintner of London. The details are given by Derek Thom in Investigating Penn and are as follows:

> "all that parcel of land in the parish of Penn containing two acres more or less and being reputed to be part of Trescott Grange ground and called Nether Heath together with the ironwork and furnace called Trescott grange furnace erected or being part of the said two acres. All those three water corn mills in the same parish called Trescott Mills. And all houses, edifices barnes stables cartilages and Millhomes... and all ways waters water courses streams of water pools ponds dams banks...to said mills ..."

Thomas's youngest son, Philip (1653-1716), bought all of his father's ironworks in this area in 1669. His purchase related to blast furnaces, forges and slitting mills. Grange was valued at £2800. This sum was made up of outstanding debts and money given for materials, as well as for carriage. Thomas Hatton of Dalicote owed £8-19-4 and £669-6-4 was in John Shaw's hands, as money paid on account for "wood cutting, cording and coling charcoles".

The Foleys' resolve had been tested a few years earlier over their right of access to the furnace site. The Earl of Dorset had inherited the Lordship of Trescott from his kinsman, Sir Richard Leveson. The Earl attempted to extract £500 per annum for passage over his land. The Foleys had answered by offering to sell the furnace to the Earl for £600, together with a pair of corn mills worth £12 per annum. Presumably they won their argument, but whether they continued to pay as little as four shillings and four pence a year for access is not known. Eventually Sir Walter Wrottesley purchased the Lordship of Trescott from the Earl and thus began this family's long association with these lands, which was to last until 1950.

The furnace, as we have seen, produced pig iron. The pigs were then passed onto forges such as those at the Heath in Wombourne and Swin at Swindon, which shaped the metal into bars. The bars were then passed on to slitting mills such as that at The Hyde, where rods were produced. Nailfactors bought the rods and supplied the cottagers who were based in villages like Wombourne and the Gornals. It was they who produced hand-made nails, returning them to the nailfactor for a pittance, who then marketed them.

Grange was not always in blast (e.g. it 'stood' in 1664, 1669 and 1672) as production always depended upon demand. It would have produced some 400 tons per year between 1692-7. In 1668 it made 605 tons of coldshort quality and in one year was credited with producing over 800 tons.

It is almost by accident that we know who was living in Grange Mill house in 1677. The following year James Illingworth wrote his account of "the man whose legs rotted off". John Duncalfe had led a dissolute life and had been given a prison term for stealing his master's iron, but he was released claiming to be sick. He continued in his old ways and stole a bible from Humphrey Babb's Grange Mill house. He asked Humphrey's wife, Margaret, for some food and drink, as he was on his way from Codsall, his parents' home, to his work and lodgings in Kingswinford. Whilst Margaret was getting his food he stole her bible, selling it to John Downing's maid at Heath forge in Wombourne for 3 shillings. His actions soon became public knowledge. He denied the accusation of theft and said if he was lying then God would let his legs drop off. They did and he repented before he died.

The Babbs must have been quite well-to-do artisans/furnace managers for they could not only read, but are credited as living at the Grange Mill house. A further reference to the Babbs is found in the Penn parish register, which records the death in 1666 of "Old Bab of the Grange Furnace". By giving his abode he is singled out as being a man of standing in the local community. There is one other later reference remembering this important family and this is found in the 1843 tythe survey when field number 900, alongside the Smestow running north to Trescott ford, is recorded as Babbs Meadow.

It is likely that the Babbs lived at one of the cottages and that this was the Mill house. As we have seen there was a community living around Grange furnace and mill. The parish registers provide more detailed evidence for the seventeenth and eighteenth centuries. Thomas the son of "widow Phillips of ye furnace" was baptised at the parish church on 6th April 1641; James Wiresdale, son of Francis and Mary was baptised in May 1718. Oher baptisms followed: on 6th April 1724, Hannah daughter of John and Ann Hawkins; on 7th July 1726 John, son of William and Mary Carter; on 15th November 1734 Joseph, son of Robant and Esther Rostance. The death of Thomas Smyth in 1666 is also recorded.

Of the other buildings on site the farmhouse with its two lower extensions is the most impressive. Its frontage, with the modern additions removed, displays similar features to that of Langley Hall in Langley Road, Lower Penn. Both are early Georgian in character with a central doorway, multi-paned windows balanced to left and right, servants' quarters hidden in the attic, a deep cool cellar on the left of the building with sandstone and brick setlases (benches) for the storing of dairy produce and a separate chamber for hanging meat and game, tall chimney breasts slightly extending beyond the line of the roof, simple brick decoration under the eaves and a brick drip course above the first-floor windows. In Langley's case a second drip course lies beneath the first-floor windows, but this can only be seen briefly at the rear of Furnace Grange as extensions hide this aspect. Langley Hall is a building dating back to the early Georgian period whilst another local farmhouse, the remodelled Orton Hall at Orton, dates from the Wrottesley improvements of 1754. A grander White Cross farmhouse at Orton dates from 1710. So, Grange Furnace dates from at least this early Georgian period. There are two features in the main body of the building which are worthy of specific attention. The flagstones in the hallway are of limestone and the link with the furnace flux is obvious. A second feature is the lock on the doorway to the cellar. Crudely constructed, but effective, these features might suggest a slightly earlier date.

The frontage of the farmhouse is in three parts, with what looks like a slightly higher Queen Anne or Georgian house in the middle of lower plainer buildings to left (dairy and saddle room) and right (kitchen). The brickwork in each building is of the hand-made irregular variety (2.5 x 9.5 x 4.5 inches with a degree of error e.g. some bricks measure 2.5 x 9.75 x 4.625 inches), probably made on the spot from clay dug on the farm. The brickwork is perhaps best displayed in the rear of the property. Which building came first is difficult to determine, but they were probably erected at the same time as the brickwork seems to be tied in? The extended chimney breast design on the central building has also been tied in to the lower buildings' roof line. A similar conundrum arises at the former Penn Children's hospital site on Penn Road, Upper Penn, where the once grand Georgian farmhouse of the Ianns family displays two fronts of different heights.

Dr King writing in *The Blackcountryman* magazine provides us with the sequence of events over the ownership of Grange during the years 1674-1708. Philip Foley was an entrepreneur and he realised he could get a better return and free up capital by leasing some of his works. In 1674 he leased Grange to a London based partnership of Sir Clement Clerke and Alderman John Foorth. They suffered from financial problems and in the coming years various partnerships ran Grange Furnace in association with other works. When the lease was up in 1692 Philip Foley along with his brother Paul, who had strong interests in the Forest of Dean's ironworks, entered into a partnership with Wheeler and Avenant and Grange was included in the package. Further changes were made in 1698 when Richard Wheeler took over a few plants including Grange, but by 1703 he was bankrupt. Finally in 1708 Philip Foley sold the furnace for conversion to a corn mill for £400, with a proviso that an

Jordan family vaults behind the chancel at St Bartholomew's

extra £400 be paid if the furnace remained in production. It was certainly working in the 1720s and was to continue until the 1770s.

It may be that the 1708 sale marks the date for the building of the present house and mill.

Another family dominates the later years of iron-working. The Jordans (sometimes spelt with an 'e', Jorden) were operating Grange and nearby Heath forge by the 1740s. The family vaults lie behind the chancel at St Bartholomew's Church in Upper Penn. They tell us that William Jorden of Grange Furnace died in his 84th year in the year of our Lord 1752, and his wife Susannah in 1759. Their offspring Thomas (died Sept 15th 1803 aged 66) and his wife, Mary (died November 11th 1818 aged 64), began raising their own family at Grange Furnace, rather than at Furnace Grange, showing that there were still industrial interests. Further evidence of ironworking is linked with Dimmingsdale wharf on the southern portion of the Staffordshire and Worcestershire Canal Navigation, which was open by

November of 1770. This would have facilitated the transport of goods to and from the furnace, as well as being an access point for the transhipment of coal from Ettingshall and Bilston, via Goldthorn Hill and Coalway and Langley Lanes (Roads). The canal was fully operational between Stourport on the River Severn and Great Haywood on the Trent and Mersey canal by 1772. However, by this time the new coking technologies of the Black Country coalfield had heralded the end of Lower Penn's iron industry. Farming had increased in importance with ready markets for produce in the expanding towns of the Black Country.

The Jordans would have known the Georgian-style residence, have sat in the dining room and relaxed in the parlour, slept in the feather beds and been supported by a small number of servants, who slept in the attic. Of Thomas and Mary's twelve children born between 1773 and 1796, two are of particular interest. The youngest child, William Stubbs Jordan, turned to farming at Furnace Grange, later taking on the 220-acre Manor Farm in Lower Penn as a tenant of the Duke of Sutherland. In 1851 he employed 15 labourers. He died at the then grand old age of 82 in 1879 having benefited from the 'Golden Age' of British farming. His daughter Mary farmed first at the Manor Farm in Lower Penn, but after her husband died the Duke of Sutherland's agent refused to let her run the farm. Little did he appreciate the resilience of the Jordan strain. She moved to Orchards and showed what she could do. Her son, Bill Blewitt, farmed there until his death in the 1990s. Members of the family, though with a different surname, are still found at a local farm beyond the parish boundary.

Not all the sons in a large family could work on the farm. William's brother, Edward Stubbs Jorden, is the second person of interest for he fought in the Peninsular War against Napoleon and survived. He was baptised in the parish church of St Bartholomew and like other families before them the Jordens would have had to make the long trek along to The Roughs and Dimmingsdale, before climbing to Lower Penn hamlet and the Springhill ridge. A further journey along the Penn Road and Vicarage Lane was needed before the church was reached. Unlike their labourers they would have travelled by trap and cart.

Edward was baptised in 1780. He enlisted in The King's Own Regiment of Staffordshire militia in 1807. He was posted as ensign. Soon the militia were quartered at Windsor, where we are told, he moved "in the highest society" and was offered a lieutenancy in the Guards. It is to his credit that "he transferred at his own request, giving up the easy life of a home-based militia for a regiment of the line". This was the era of the Revolutionary and Napoleonic Wars when Britain was fighting France almost without interruption from 1793-1815. Within a year of joining up, Edward Jorden transferred to the Cameronians, the 26th Regiment of foot. He was to serve in the Peninsula (Spain and Portugal). In 1808 the Cameronians, a lowland Scottish Regiment, required a further 10 lieutenants as numbers of all ranks were increased. In the event four promotions came from within and Edward, an outsider, was 'made up without purchase'. This meant that he did not buy his commission, but was raised in rank because of his ability.

He first served with the second battalion in Glasgow before sailing with them from Grouville, Jersey on 23rd June 1811. There were 618 in the ranks, 21 drummers, 34 sergeants, and 38 officers, all in three transports. They entered the Tagus after 10 days and disembarked a day later at Lisbon. They took part in the blockade of Cuidad Rodrigo and in the affairs near Aldea de Ponte. 1812 found much sickness in the regiment and many deaths. A shortage of blankets and diarrhoea were particular problems. The Cameronians moved back to Lisbon before embarking for Gibraltar, where they took over garrison duties. There was an outbreak of fever in the town and many lives were lost, but Edward survived.

Lieutenant Edward Jorden remained with the regiment until October of 1817 when he retired on half pay due to ill health. His record shows that he commented he would have preferred full pay. Returning to his home county, he took up residence in Penn, living in a house on the north side of Penn Road between the Roebuck and what is now Pennhouse Avenue. He became High Constable for Seisdon South and afterwards for Seisdon North, which included the town of Wolverhampton. The role of the High Constable was to ensure that law and order was maintained. He would have had to see that there were enough petty constables and to advise the magistrates of any difficulties, which might lead to reading the Riot Act.

With the passing of the Great Reform Act of 1832, which first gave Wolverhampton the right to return a member of parliament, election times were potentially times of civil unrest, as most males (and no females) were unable to vote. Voting was conducted in public at one of several booths around the town and huge crowds turned out to jeer and challenge the well-to-do. There was trouble in 1832, but events were to prove that the system of Petty Constable/High Constable/Magistrate was outdated. There was a more serious breakdown of law and order at the 1835 election. Huge numbers had gathered at the close of the poll on Wednesday 27th May on High Green (Queens Square) and in the Market Place. Constant shouting, jeering, spitting and the throwing of mud and stones meant that those with the vote were intimidated and in some cases failed to cast their ballot. Whilst Edward had eventually persuaded the magistrates to swear in additional petty constables and deputy constables providing a total force of about 39, most were too frightened to appear. In any case by the evening of the 27th there were 4000 protesters. Edward eventually persuaded Mr Clare, one of the magistrates to send to Dudley for the dragoons and by that evening Mr Clare read the Riot Act from the balcony of the Swan Inn in High Green. The mounted troops eventually had to be brought out of their billets as they were ordered to clear the streets. Shots were fired, whilst some of the mob gained access to St Peter's churchyard and even to the roof of the church itself. The Riot Act was again read on both Thursday and Friday by Mr Briscoe. The Secretary of State at the Home Department (Home Office) ordered an inquiry, which was led by Sir Frederick Adair Rose.

The expanding industrial towns had outgrown the hundred system of local government. In 1843 Gilbert Hogg was appointed Chief Constable, the police force being further strengthened in 1848 when Wolverhampton was incorporated as a borough. Edward, using his title of Captain Edward Jorden, now filled the office of Inspector of Weights and Measures for the southern division of the county. He continued to discharge this duty until within a few days of his death.

His army pension was worth £80 a year and this, together with his other income, allowed him to live modestly the life of a gentleman. In private life he was much respected. His obituary in the

Wolverhampton Chronicle tells of his kindness to the poor of his native parish and it refers to his limited means. Edward appears to have remained unmarried, but like his younger brother, William Stubbs Jordan, he was to live to a ripe old age. He kept one servant. He died from bronchitis on 17th July 1863 aged 83 years.

To return to the story of Furnace Grange, the 1851 census unsurprisingly showed the cottages occupied by agricultural labourers and their families. The house then listed as Grange Mill was inhabited by John Miller, his wife Ann, and their 2 daughters and 3 sons. John was a tenant farmer of Lord Wrottesley managing 300 acres and running the mill. He employed 12 labourers as well as a groom and two servants who lived in. From this time and for the next 40 years first John and then Joseph Miller were millers here. A roughly carved stone commemorating John's son William, and dated 1866 when he was 34 has been reset into one of the interior walls of the mill building. This may refer to the date when John and family left the farm for at the 1871 census he is aged 73, described as a retired farmer and living with his wife, daughter, son and 2 grandchildren in part of Trescott Grange. Joseph is listed between 1873-1892 as a steam miller and farmer living at The Grange. The Millers

Possibly the date that John Miller retired to Trescott Grange and William his son commemorated the move

moved with the times and transferred most of their milling operations to Corn Hill in Wolverhampton, where they built a steam mill.

With the passage of time and the loss of living witnesses as well as the plethora of terms – The Grange, Grange Hall, The Hall, Trescott Grange, Grange Furnace, Furnace Grange – it is sometimes difficult to distinguish which family lived where. The problem is further compounded by tenancy agreements and at times the use of farm bailiffs by the Wrottesley estate. So the relationship between Furnace and Trescott Grange in the second half of the nineteenth and early twentieth century can be problematic. We do know however that in 1851 Henry Harris was the tenant at Trescott employing some 21 labourers as well as wagoners, a groom and a shepherd to farm his 640 acres of Lord Wrottesley's land. The Harrises left the farm in 1854. The Wrottesleys seemed to have changed their policy for by 1871 both farms were managed by farm bailiffs. John Shuker from Childs Ercall was at Trescott Grange, sharing the building with John Miller, whilst Joseph Burrard was the bailiff at Furnace Grange.

Thomas Kirby was the farmer at Trescott which possibly included both farms from about 1896 until 1916. Frank Howard Jeavons was the next tenant of Lord Wrottesley. Where once there had been three mills, the remaining Grange mill ceased working in the 1920s as economics determined that flour would be produced in large industrial mills driven by either steam or electricity. Frank survived through the most of the depression years, but by 1934 he had lost the battle and a farm sale was

Thomas Stanley Inett

organised to sell off his equipment. John Nock of Nock & Joseland of Queen Street, Wolverhampton, auctioneers, valuers and estate agents, became tenant at Trescott Grange in 1934 and in the same year Thomas Stanley Inett became tenant at Furnace Grange. He came from Hall End Lane Farm at Pattingham. To increase their farm income, Thomas Stanley and his father had sold produce, particularly fruit, at their Wolverhampton market stall. He had been offered Rudge Farm rent free for a year, but instead he chose to pay the Wrottesley Estate annually 7 shillings and six pence (37.5p) an acre for the 250 or so acres of Furnace Grange, knowing that the soils were of good quality, the aspect of the land favourable, and that there was the added advantage of the Smestow Brook running through its land.

The Baron's agent was Chris Hatton and he quickly complained to Thomas Stanley Inett that he was not keeping any cattle. He offered to find him a farmer who would pay him for allowing cattle to graze. Times were hard and he did not have the money to buy a herd of store cattle, but he knew that he could build one up over time, replacing animals as they went to market. He therefore replied that the only cattle that he would graze would be his own. When he had made enough money, he began buying Herefords and followed with Shorthorns and Aberdeen Angus. They were transported into Herbert Street Goods station and walked on the hoof to Trescott throughout the 1930s and 1940s. Tettenhall station, on the Wombourn line, was used to import cattle, as well as seed potatoes from Scotland. Fertilisers were also delivered to this Great Western Railway (GWR)station, the Inetts having to unload the rail wagon. Thomas Stanley Inett was a hard-working and shrewd farmer, who step by step laid the foundations for a successful farm. As in all farming families his children helped run the farm: John, Bill and their sister Angela all had their jobs to complete. The family photograph at left shows the boys driving a 1918 Austin metal-wheeled tractor when they were about 12 and 14 years of age. They had persuaded a relative to give them the machine.

The war years gave British farming a much-needed boost, as vastly increased food production was essential if Britain was to beat the U-boat blockade. Farmers were now under the control of the Ministry of Food and the dreaded County Committees. The availability of manpower was a key issue. Furnace Grange benefited from the work of Italian prisoners of war in draining some low-lying fields between the Smestow and Black Brooks. The war caused other difficulties. Furnace Grange lay on the direct flight path of RAF Perton's main runway – Runway Nr1, which had a southwest trajectory. Although there was officially no night flying, waves of enemy aircraft regularly passed overhead on their way to and from Merseyside. The family spent many nights in the damp cellar.

Thomas Stanley Inett purchased Furnace Grange from the Wrottesleys in 1950.

Today John Inett, his son Christopher and three workers produce our food on this busy farm. There is always a presence and no detail goes by unseen. These days the family lands are extensive, some 800 acres stretch away towards Pattingham. 75% of the land is used for arable cash crops. The remaining land is down to pasture and

Inett boys on farm tractor, 1918

fodder crops. 1000 sheep over-winter here feeding on stubble turnips, the ground being quickly prepared for their sowing after the harvest, so that they are ready by mid-October. Pasture is also rented out to other farms for the winter grazing of cattle.

At one time, as is the case on other local farms, mangold wurzels were grown and harvested as cattle feed. They have gone out of fashion, because they cannot be mechanically harvested without bruising. Another crop that has vanished in the new millennium is sugar beet, simply because government policy allowed the two local refining plants to close, thereby concentrating production in East Anglia. True that it cost 8 pence a pound to produce sugar from cane, and 24 pence a pound through beet, but to have kept one beet-processing plant in the West Midlands may have been strategically sound.

Hoopoe

Furnace Grange does much to encourage and support wildlife. A recent bird survey found 66 species of British birds, many of them nesting. Of the more unusual species are the hobby, which likes to hunt in early morning and from late afternoon until dusk. It will both glide and hover and can be seen hunting the Smestow for dragonflies and other insects. It will also take small birds. It likes to nest in a discarded crow's nest and prefers woodland. John Inett has indeed been fortunate for he has seen on one occasion the hoopoe, with its striking pink crest and black and white barred wings. John has also counted a flock of 22 yellowhammers in one location. These birds were once a common sight singing at the top of our hedgerows and nesting at ground level on a hedgerow bank or ditch. Flocks of fieldfares are regularly seen during the winter, staying for about a month before moving off to find another food source. The day I visited John we saw the black sleek neck of the Brent goose on the rented-out carp pond. We talked of the species which once could be seen on these lands – the common, grey or English partridge and the hare – that are now gone and truly missed, but not forgotten. Even the whir of the red-legged or French partridge is rare these days. When John's father came to Furnace Grange there were still trout in the Smestow, but the foul discharges of Courtaulds factory had a profound effect on the river. One day the waters were normal, the next day they could be white, or blue or a reddish colour. Fortunately the Smestow is a much cleaner river these days providing a range of habitats for a varied wildlife. Of the new arrivals the white little egret is a welcome addition as it wanders the Smestow's shores.

Until recently when government funding was withdrawn there was a permissive path for horse riders, a scheme which worked to the benefit of the local community and which reflected the forward-thinking and generous nature of this farming family. In this post-Brexit age there is an air of uncertainty, but those at Furnace Grange are ready to take up the challenges in the best interest of British farming and our environment.

Chapter 16
Miscellaneous pictures

A correction – Fletchers' shop

This is now a private residence, lying just off the Common on the west side of Sedgley Road. The photograph as shown on p.89 of *Penn: Explored, Explained & Remembered* erroneously labelled as Fletchers' in fact shows Nightingales Stores, which lay higher up on Sedgley Rd. This is also now a private residence.

Another correction

P. 41 of *The Smestow: Wolverhampton's River* - William Shenton was an occupier of Trescott Grange, and not of Furnace Grange.

Confluence of Black Brook and Smestow Brook at the western end of Lower Penn parish.

Correction: geological map on page 66 should read Etruria Marl of Upper Coal Measures and not of middle coal measures.

Georgian Iann's Farm – Penn Hospital building, as mentioned in Chapter 15.

List of illustrations

Angus Dunphy grew up on the Orton Hills at the end of the Second World War, where his parents provided a happy childhood home. From an early age he and his three brothers roamed across much of Penn and Wombourne, and a Christmas present of a bike at age seven made expeditions over the South Staffordshire countryside a joy. He trained as a teacher in Bangor, north Wales, where he met his wife Gail, a miner's daughter from the Rhymney Valley. They married in 1967. He taught for 20 years in schools in the Black Country before taking on the headship of Fitzalan High School, Cardiff, a large inner-city multi-ethnic comprehensive serving the Bay area. He was awarded the OBE in 2001 for services to education and retired in 2004. He retired for the second time in 2016 from his role as an education consultant, and he is currently a churchwarden. He has a son and a daughter and two grandchildren.

Writing about the Penn country is his attempt to keep his roots. This is his sixteenth book.

Other books by Angus Dunphy

Out of print
A Geography of Wombourne and Lower Penn
Angus Dunphy's Penn
Memories of Penn and District
Out and About in Penn and District
Penn and Ink
Over and Nether Penn
Penn to Paper
Penn in Print
A Millennium History of Lower Penn
A Penny For Your Thoughts: As we were in Lower Penn 1894-1972
From Bhylls to Pennstones: As we were in Lower Penn 1972-1992
Tales From Penn Forge
Penn: Forest, Field, Fireside
The Smestow: Wolverhampton's River

A few copies of the following are still available, at time of printing of this book:

Penn & District: Explored, Explained & Remembered (£12.50 including P&P)

from:

8 Chestnut Close
Dinas Powys
Vale of Glamorgan
CF64 4TJ

E: angusdunphy@yahoo.co.uk